THE ARNOLD WAY

Please return / renew this item by last date shown. Books may also be renewed by phone or the Internet.

Northamptonshire Libraries and Information Service

Northamptonshire County Council

www.northamptonshire.gov.uk/catalogue

The Arnold Way

© Copyright 2008 Anthony J. Boyce

Published by
British Deaf History Society Publications
288 Bedfont Lane
Feltham
Middlesex TW14 9NU

a branch of

British Deaf History Society
11-13 Wilson Patten Road
Warrington
Cheshire
ENGLAND
WA1 1PG

All rights reserved

No part of this book may be reproduced by any
means, or transmitted, or translated into a machine
language or any similar form without the written consent
of the publisher and the author.

British Library Cataloguing Data

ISBN 978-1-902427-32-4

Editor: Anthony J. Boyce
Art Editor: Christopher Marsh

Front cover photos: Thomas Arnold, Hugh N. Dixon and Frederick Ince-Jones

The Arnold Way

A brief history and pictorial record of the
Northampton High School for the Deaf
1868 - 1945

Anthony J. Boyce

The Arnold Way

Note:-

Where group photographs or pictures are shown, names of persons are to be read from left to right unless otherwise stated.

Contents

Acknowledgements vi

Introduction vii

Chapter 1.   The Arnold Era (1868 - 1884) 1

Chapter 2.   The Dixon Era (1885 - 1908) 11

Chapter 3.   The Ince-Jones Era (1909 - 1929) 17

Chapter 4.   The Prime of Ince-Jones (1930 - 1938) 41

Chapter 5.   Out-door Activities 61

Chapter 6.   The Finale 81

Appendices   A1. Staff of the Northampton High School for the Deaf (1868 - 1945)   95

              A2. List of ex-pupils of the Northampton High School for the Deaf   96

              A3. School Roll of Honour 100

              A4. Prospectus of the Northampton High School for the Deaf   102

              A5. Photographic Gallery . . . . .
                   (a) Spring Hill School Groups 104
                   (b) Spring Hill School Cricket Teams . . . 109
                   (c) Spring Hill School Football Teams . . . 111
                   (d) The Pritchard Photographic Collection . . 113
                   (e) The Philip E. Gibbons Photographic Collection . 117

              A6. Notes 121

              A7. Sketched plans of the Spring Hill premises . . . 130

              A8. Old Pupils' Contributions 133

Illustrations 141

References 144

Acknowledgements

We acknowledge our most heartfelt thanks to Mr. George Drewry, the late Dr. Bernard Pitcher, Mr. Philip Gibbons, Mr. Derek Pritchard and Mrs. Elaine Lavery for their invaluable contribution, help, advice and photographs, to Mr. Christopher Marsh for his care and thought in art work and design that went into the production of this book and to Mr. Richard Goulden for proofreading.

Special thanks also are given to the following people for their contribution to this book:

Ian Depledge
Geoffrey Eagling
John A. Hay, M.B.E.
David Hyslop, O.B.E.
Ian Stewart (Doddridge Chapel, Northampton)
Ian Urquhart (Spurs Deaf Club)

We also wish to record our thanks to the following for permission to use material for this book:

Richard Goulden (Spurs Deaf Club)
The Staff, Local History Studies, Northampton Central Public Library
The Staff, Northamptonshire Record Office
Northamptonshire Record Society
The Staff, R.N.I.D. Library, London
The National Archives, Kew
The Staff, Doncaster Archives
Doncaster Deaf Trustees
The Staff, John Rylands Library, Manchester University
British Library, London

Finally our grateful appreciation and thanks to the Constance E. Travis Charitable Trust and Maud Elkington Charitable Trust for their grants that make this book *The Arnold Way* possible and to the British Deaf History Society for its support and help in securing the grants.

Introduction

The Northampton Oral High School for the Deaf sited in the heart of England was once a well-known landmark whose history little seems to be known even in circles closely connected with the education of the deaf. This unique private school for the deaf was established in 1868 and ran for 77 years before its closure in 1945. Its founder was the Reverend Thomas Arnold (1816 – 1897), who earned the title "A Giver of Speech". Much has been written about Arnold, one of the most quoted names in the history of education of the deaf, for he was mainly responsible for the rapid spread of the oral method in the United Kingdom in the last 25 years of his life through his publications.

There is and has long been much controversy on methods of teaching the deaf. While the question is not debated in this book, for those readers who may not be familiar with the three methods of communication used in British schools for the deaf during the Victorian era and the first half of the twentieth century, these methods are outlined. The oral method was that which used only speech and lipreading as a means of communication with deaf children, that is, the Arnold way. The manual method used fingerspelling and signs, the aim being to get thought across to deaf children's minds. The combined method made use of both the oral and manual methods, with the idea of suiting the method to a deaf child rather than the deaf child to the method.

The development of the Northampton school is based on three eras and each era represents the head-cum-proprietor of the School, namely, the Reverend Thomas Arnold (1868 - 1884), Mr. Hugh N. Dixon (1885 - 1908) and Mr. Frederick Ince-Jones (1909 - 1945). Each succeeding head followed the Arnold way of teaching speech, lipreading and language although with some modifications.

Very little research has been carried out in detail on British private schools for the deaf during the Victorian period and the first fifty years of the 20th century. Although the recently published *The Lady in Green* is a biography of Miss Mary Hare, it was the first such attempt to trace the historical development of her private school for the deaf. In 1911, it was recorded that there were only 25 British private schools for the deaf and, in every one of them, pupils were taught by means of speech and lipreading. Each private school was run for profit and was the property of the head teacher, who was free to set up its own school curriculum. It received no grants at all from the government. It was free from government interference. After the passing of the 1902 Education Act, the only real opportunity for British secondary education for the deaf was provided by a few of those private schools outside the national educational state system. Government inspections on private schools for the deaf were rarely carried out, and so no adequate history of them will ever be told. As a matter of fact, the only school for the deaf until 1945 recognised by the Minister of Education as providing secondary education for the deaf was the Northampton High School for the Deaf. Complete official records of any private school for the deaf have yet to be found, which makes it very difficult to study its historical development and organisation. Thus what has been done in *The Arnold Way* is the compilation of all the bits and pieces of information so as to give an idea of the historical development of the Northampton Oral High School for the Deaf as a record for posterity.

The Northampton High School for the Deaf was located on five different sites, namely, 21 Primrose Hill (1868 - 1877), Fairview House, Cliftonville (1878 - 1885), 25 St. Paul's Road (1886), Wickham House at 23 East Park Parade, Kingsthorpe (1887 - 1911) and Spring Hill, Cliftonville (1912 - 1945). Today, Fairview House is no longer in existence but the other four houses survive. Spring Hill House is at present a certified Grade 2 building.

Extracts from some ex-pupils' brief accounts found in various magazines and their old photographs have been inserted in *The Arnold Way*. Mr. Philip E. Gibbons, the oldest known surviving ex-pupil of Spring Hill School, aged 95 years, and the late Dr. Bernard L. Pitcher, the first British born deaf person to be awarded the doctorate degree, helped to identify pupils and staff in some old well-preserved photographs and pictures from their old albums and also gave some invaluable verbal information about their days at school. Also included is George Drewry's lively hand-written manuscript which gives an account of his days at Spring Hill from the junior's viewpoint during the Second World War. Mr. Derek Pritchard, whose father and uncle were ex-pupils, Lyonel and Kenneth Pritchard respectively, kindly allowed their old photographs taken from 1917 to 1932 to be included. It is indeed difficult to know to which of the many friends and families the original negatives belong to. Many times the same picture is repeated in different family albums and magazines for the deaf. The origins, or ownership, or copyright-consent, if known, are given the tag of courtesy. There are some photographs taken by unidentified photographers and owners during the first three decades of the twentieth century and, although attempts have been made to trace them but to no avail, the author wishes to acknowledge the fact that the copyright for most of them has expired. Much appreciation and special thanks are given to the above named contributors for without their help *The Arnold Way* would not have been produced.

The author and Bernard Pitcher on his 90th birthday on September 18 1999 at Worthing, West Sussex

Philip E. Gibbons and his photo albums, 2008

A complete set of *The Teacher of the Deaf* issues from 1903 to 1954 also provided some historical pieces of information. Lyonel Pritchard's rare set of *Spring Hill School Magazine* issues from 1930 to 1945 contains a mine of information. Both sets have been donated to the National Archives of the Deaf, Warrington, under the auspices of the British Deaf History Society.

Lyonel Pritchard, a toolmaker's engineer, 1955
Courtesy of Derek Pritchard

No deposit of official records of the said School exists in either the Northamptonshire Record Office or the Local History Studies of Northampton Central Public Library, but recently a typed manuscript *Awakened* by Mr. Frederick Ince-Jones was discovered and preserved at the Northamptonshire Record Office. It was mainly addressed to the general public on details of the problems of the deaf including some examples from his school in Northampton as a way of illustration. It was completed in July 1953 and was meant for publication, but the following year saw the death of Mr. Ince-Jones and it was shelved. It was given to the Northamptonshire Record Society in 1976. Some extracts from *Awakened* are reproduced in *The Arnold Way* by kind permission of the Northamptonshire Record Society.

The opening statement in the preface of *Awakened* is taken from Mr. Somerset Maugham's "*A Writer's Notebook*" on page 62, and it reads:-

The only means of improving the race is by elimination of the unfit. All methods which tend to their preservation – education of the blind and of deaf-mutes – can only cause degeneration.

Mr. Frederick Ince-Jones's *Awakened* was his answer to Mr. Somerset Maugham's *ridiculous* statement. Some relevant extracts have been taken from *Awakened* and appropriately inserted in *The Arnold Way*, especially on his attempts on teaching of language and his views on the suppression of sign language.

Readers are reminded that, during Mr. Ince-Jones's headship at Spring Hill School, there were two important on-going developments, namely, the new technical development of hearing aids which provided more help to those who possessed residual hearing in terms of speech-training, and the increasing adaptation of the cinema to educational uses, which provided a new method of approach, beneficial to those who depended so much on sight. Mr. Ince-Jones, himself a distinguished botanist, embarked on experimenting with speech-teaching and language-teaching during those years and proved himself a pioneer in raising the standards of education to a higher level for deaf children. He emphasised that his pupils were not selected for their intelligence and that they were of average ability. His special asset was his ability to use language at all levels clothed in its simplicity and in style and, for deaf children, he was a language teacher for the deaf *par excellence*. For inspiration, he owed much to the Rev. Thomas Arnold as he commented in 1941:-

Arnold's portrait hangs in the big schoolroom. One of his desks is still in use, 'Though mangled, hacked and hewn, not yet destroyed.' His original language lessons – and very good they are – remain in my possession, as do his set of coloured charts ... It may therefore be maintained that Arnold's spirit still lives, not only in his books, but in the continuous stream of secondary education inspired by his teaching and going on today in his own school. He being dead yet speaketh.

The setting down of the facts, with due regard at the same time to the need for a readable and interesting narrative, has not been easy. Apologies are given for any errors or omissions, which must inevitably occur, although facts stated are as accurate as is possible.

Anthony J. Boyce
October 2008

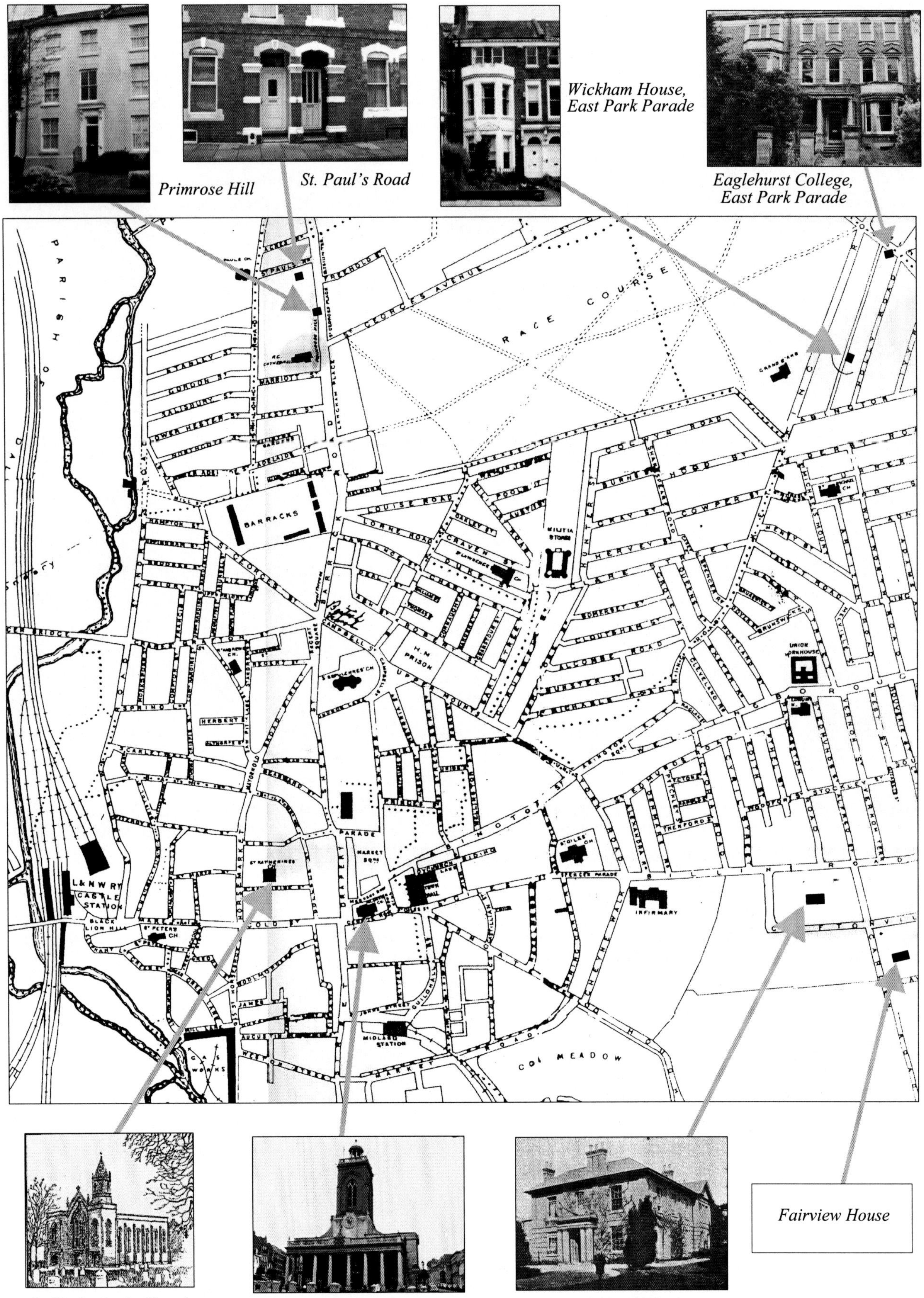

The Arnold Way

Primrose Hill

St. Paul's Road

Wickham House, East Park Parade

Eaglehurst College, East Park Parade

St. Katharine's Church

All Saints' Church

Spring Hill

Fairview House

Map of Northampton town
*Courtesy of Local History Studies, Northampton Central Public Library
with the additions of photos by the author*

Chapter 1

The Arnold Era (1868 – 1884)

The history of the Northampton High School for the Deaf starts with a brief biography of the Reverend Thomas Arnold the founder of the school. He was born in Gracehill in County Antrim, Ireland, on April 28 1816. His family was concerned with the business of cabinet-making, but Thomas Arnold chose a teaching career, starting at a local boys' school. It was during this time that he first met a young deaf cabinet maker, James Beatty, who had been taught at Claremont Institution for the Deaf and Dumb, Dublin. James used signs and fingerspelling. Arnold tried to communicate with him by means of gestures and writing, but to no avail.

Arnold left Ireland for Manchester and, whilst there, he was shown an advertisement in the *Manchester Guardian* for a post of an assistant teacher at the Yorkshire Institution for the Deaf and Dumb in Doncaster (abbreviated YIDD). He applied for the job and was accepted by Mr. Charles Baker, the headmaster of the YIDD, in 1840. In Mr. Arnold's book *Reminiscences of Forty Years*, he wrote about his first day at Doncaster:-

... I was conducted over the school and saw the teachers at work in their classes. These were taught by signs, the manual alphabet and writing after printed or written lessons. It was exceedingly interesting. The scholars had evidently learned that I was likely to be the new teacher. Already a sign which became my new school name was found for me, and was at once adopted, passed about and oft repeated. There were also sharp criticisms on my person, my disposition, and fitness. More than one hundred scholars were present and as I glanced over them I realised their sad privations. My sympathy was deeply moved, and for the first time the burden was felt of being their teacher. To instruct them would be difficult and trying, and would make the greatest demands on patience and perseverance. In truth such self denial as was never required in teaching the hearing. But I was young, hopeful, and felt something of the enterprising courage which anticipates the pleasure of mastered difficulties. Upon the whole the verdict of my scholars was in my favour. Mr. Baker did not conceal the real difficulties of the task, or that they would be chiefly of myself. This was afterwards proved to be too true.

Mr. William Sleight, Arnold's close friend and fellow-teacher at the YIDD, said that Arnold found the manual method of communication difficult to apply in a natural and fluent manner.

As no oral classes existed at the YIDD, Mr. Baker wished Mr. Arnold to attempt the teaching of articulation to some of the pupils and sent him to the Liverpool School for the Deaf, of which Mr. James Rhind was the headmaster. At Liverpool, Mr. Arnold saw a class taught by the articulation method for only one hour. On his return to Doncaster, he was given an oral class, but found teaching deaf children to speak very difficult. As the sign-manual method of communication was chiefly used, the conditions were not favourable to running a class on an oral basis. Progress was slow, but one boy, George Cocking, articulated and lipread well. One day, while on business in Doncaster, the Rev. Cocking called at the YIDD to see his son George. When they met, George said *"O father, how do you do?"*. It was the first time his father heard him speak. Since then, Arnold became a convert to the oral system even though, whilst teaching deaf children to speak, he found it very trying.

After three years, he left the YIDD to study for Church ministry and became a minister. Within the next sixteen years, he focussed on his clerical duties in Burton-on-Trent and

Birmingham. In 1848 he married Sarah Simpson. During that time, he studied the practice of teaching speech, using the *American Annals* and some foreign books, and he made notes for future use. He had not taught any deaf child since he left Doncaster. In 1858 Arnold and his wife sailed to Australia and, whilst there, Sir Thomas Holt, an influential gentleman from Sydney, paid Arnold to teach his sixteen year-old deaf son, Frederick Holt, on a private basis along oral lines. Frederick Holt became deaf from scarlet fever at the age of 8. There was at this time no school for deaf children in Australia. After a year Arnold developed a serious spinal complaint and he was advised to return to England. Returning to England, the Arnolds were joined by Frederick Holt and his brother. In England, Arnold's health was greatly improved and in due course he accepted an offer to be the pastor of the Doddridge Chapel in Northampton.

It was on May 13 1860 that the Reverend Thomas Arnold and his wife, Sarah, arrived at Northampton and settled temporarily in Adelaide Street. Then they moved to a 3-storied house at 21 Primrose Hill and it was there that Frederick Holt, aged 18, was received as Arnold's first private deaf and dumb boarding pupil on August 19 1860. In Arnold's *Education of the Deaf* in 1882, he wrote:-

In 1860 I brought a youth from Australia, whose speech I restored. He had almost lost it through scarlet fever. He became able to converse freely with others, and happily his hearing afterwards returned. I may say he was the occasion of my taking up and developing the oral method of teaching. I had no assistance from any other teacher.

21 Primrose Hill, Northampton, arrowed. 2008

Frederick left in 1862 to join his uncle in Harrogate, Yorkshire. *(See Notes 5.)* During the next six years, the Rev. Arnold continued his local clerical work and contributed much to the growth of local schools and undertook some teaching, but was not involved with any deaf educational work.

To have an idea of the man the Rev. Thomas Arnold was, he was more than six feet tall and had a leonine head and a massive but not heavy figure, which gave him an imposing appearance. He was one of the best known and most striking personalities in the town. He had an aloofness, which made familiarity with him difficult. He was abrupt in manner. He had no patience with trivialities. He was described as an eccentric man with *a rich mellow voice*.

Meanwhile, at Leeds, Abraham Farrar was born on January 26 1861, the son of Abraham Farrar, a small landed proprietor, and Sarah Shaw. At the age of three, he became totally deaf through scarlet fever and eventually lost his speech. In *The British Deaf Times*, 1928, he wrote:-

The earliest figure I can recall is that of Charles Baker of the Doncaster Institution, who was the most important man in the profession. I had been taken by my father to see him in reference to my education, but I never went there...

Indeed, Abraham's father visited Mr. Baker as to the possibility of his son being educated along oral lines. Mr. Baker recommended him to the Rev. Thomas Arnold.

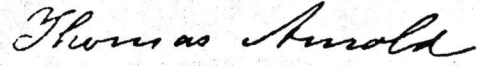

HOW THE SCHOOL BEGAN

By A. Farrar, junior, F.G.S.

Behold me a little fellow arriving with his mother on the 23rd January 1868, a few days before his seventh birthday, at the house of the Reverend Thomas Arnold at 21 Primrose Hill, half-way on the road to Kingsthorpe...

At that time there was hardly any private school for the deaf, except two kept by Mr. Van Asch and Mr. Barber, and I am not sure when they began. Private pupils were usually taken by the headmasters of the institutions and resided with them. My father heard of Mr. Arnold in a casual way as one who had experience as a teacher of the deaf, and it was with some difficulty that he was persuaded to receive me. And so the school began.

Northampton at this time was a small, old fashioned country town with only half-a-dozen churches and only two or three boot and shoe manufactories of any great size. For the next few years I was Mr. Arnold's only pupil, but life was by no means dull as his public position brought me in contact with many people of all sorts in the town and country which, I may say, by the way, was of great benefit to me, as it gave scope for my speech and lip-reading.

It was truly a challenge for Arnold, who had only less than five years' teaching experience of deaf children, and, after some hesitation, he agreed to Mr. Farrar's request that he educate Abraham on a private one-to-one oral basis. It meant that his time was divided between his public duties and his private teaching commitments. As time passed by, Abraham's progress was such that it encouraged Arnold to continue teaching him. Whilst going about it, he made an analysis on the principles of speech and language, applied them in practice and chronicled the developments made.

To master the intricacies of speech he [Arnold] *practised on his own. At night, after he had gone to rest, he was often working out the formation of sounds by lip, and tongue, and teeth, and, till she got accustomed to his method of study, Mrs. Arnold was sometimes startled from her sleep by the explosions of his mouth.*

Out of lesson hours, Arnold took Abraham everywhere with him to meet his clerical friends for discussion. Abraham's early experience at Northampton, which was *so different from that of most private schoolboys,* proved to be beneficial to him. For example, he recalled:-

... the Rev. J. T. Brown who always took delight in talking to me when a little fellow, and, as his articulation was very clear, I understood him almost better than Arnold himself.

In 1872 Arnold had his first ever pamphlet published and its title was *The Education of the Deaf and Dumb: an exposition and a review of the French* [signs and fingerspelling] *and German* [oral] *systems,* in which he strongly favoured the latter method.

In 1874, Arnold, excited by his successful progress of teaching speech and lipreading, admitted his second deaf pupil, Rollo Dixon, the younger brother of Hugh Neville Dixon, who would eventually join Arnold as his teaching assistant in 1883. *(See Notes 6.)*

On September 12 1874 Arnold gave his first public talk on *How to Teach the Dumb to Speak,* using his star pupil Abraham Farrar as an example. After a preamble on speech and sound, he said that, when he began with his pupil, he showed him by using fingers the vibration of sound in his throat.

The pupil became aware and tried to do the same. In some instances the pupil could produce the same sound and thus the foundation was laid...He [Arnold] *began with vowels and then consonants. The elements of the vowels he taught him from the motion of his lips. Of course there were modifications. These were indicated by the fingers. Short sounds were indicated by short signs, and long sounds were indicated by long signs.*

He knew how difficult was the task of teaching speech to any deaf pupil and remarked that

...it had been his [Arnold's] *good fortune to have the aid of a pupil who had the natural intelligence to surrender himself to him, and allow him to play on his organs of speech that he might learn to speak as he did....*

Then he proceeded to the teaching of language. He got Farrar to pronounce his first word and then tried to make use of it, beginning with the simplest of sentences. He began with "*I have a book.*" The pupil repeated the sentence after him. Then the conversation between Arnold and Farrar led to:-

"*What are you?*"	"*A boy*"
"*Where do you live?*"	"*At Northampton with Mr. Arnold.*"
"*What are you learning?*"	"*To speak*"
"*And what more?*"	"*Geography*"
"*What more?*"	"*Mathematics*".

By this time Farrar, thirteen years of age, had already done the first and second books of Euclid in geometry and was using Dr. Smith's books to learn Latin. In conclusion of the meeting, Arnold

... desired his pupil to read a verse from the 1st chapter of the Gospel of John in the Latin, which he did, and afterwards repeated several verses from a poem. A want of flexibility was noticeable in the youth's voice, otherwise he articulated with considerable accuracy.

In October 1875 Arnold gave another public lecture on the same subject and this time he brought in his two pupils, *both deaf but now not wholly dumb,* for demonstration purposes.

The more advanced pupil, a young gentleman of 14 [Farrar], recited the first stanza of Gray's "Elegy in a Country Churchyard"... gave the extraction of the square root from a number and the exposition of that extraction, with algebraic proof.

Present in the audience was Mr. P. Phipps, who was a Northampton Borough member and a M.P., and Arnold, after having demonstrated Farrar's attainments, had his support to ensure that the oral method should be widely circulated among the influential members of Parliament as a preference to the old system of signs and fingerspelling.

Arnold had a large library shelved in several rooms of his house. He allowed Farrar to have access to these books. Farrar's continual habit of reading books allowed him to acquire a command of language.

By the winter of 1876 Farrar took the Cambridge Local examinations and passed classics and mathematics with honours. Local and national newspapers gave reports of his success. The Prince of Wales, who would eventually become King Edward VII after the death of Queen Victoria, sent a letter of congratulations to Arnold. In the summer of 1877 Arnold and Farrar made a grand tour of Europe for two months.

Arnold and his pupils attended church service at Doddridge Church on Sundays and Farrar wrote:-

I'm usually able to understand the numbers of the hymns and such like details; but, as for the sermon, I just sit it through and hope I shall not be considered irreverent if I add that I don't greatly miss it!

As a result of the nationwide newspaper reports on Farrar's examination success, Arnold received letters from parents asking for private oral tuition for their deaf children. This prompted Arnold to take up part time work as a local minister and to concentrate fully on his teaching. The number of deaf children in his class grew and this forced Arnold to seek a larger building, and by 1877 he rented a large mansion, Fairview House, situated at Cliftonville, Northampton. He described himself as *the Master of the Middle Class for the Deaf.* At the same time Rollo Dixon left and took up a gardening career along the south coast of England.

Farrar continued his education, but was mainly taught by Mr. Beeby Thompson, F.G.S., Master of the Northampton School of Science. In 1880 he passed the South Kensington Science and Art examinations in Chemistry and Geology and received the Queen's Prize. Now he aimed for the London University Matriculation examination and had the help of two tutors, one for Science and the other for Classics, and, although both tutors had no previous knowledge of the deaf, they understood Farrar's speech. He attended the science classes at the Northampton Grammar School and found his science tutor very difficult to lipread. So the conversation on the tutor's side was carried out by writing, to which Farrar responded orally. Farrar received private tuition in Classics from an Oxford graduate, whom he found so easy to lipread. The tutors then led Farrar to join in some local societies such as the Natural History Society and the Field Club in order to get away from Arnold's *hot-house atmosphere of a secluded home life*. Thus Farrar had the opportunity of lipreading various people in all walks of life.

Regarding Farrar's speech and lipreading, Mr. Ince-Jones, who would eventually become the third head of Arnold's school, knew him well and wrote that:-

Farrar proved an apt pupil... He became a good speaker for though his speech was rather monotonous owing to lack of rhythm and similarity of vowel sounds, his consonants were so carefully pronounced that he was always intelligible and he was a good lipreader.

An extract from the *Northampton Mercury* of February 5 1881, reads:-

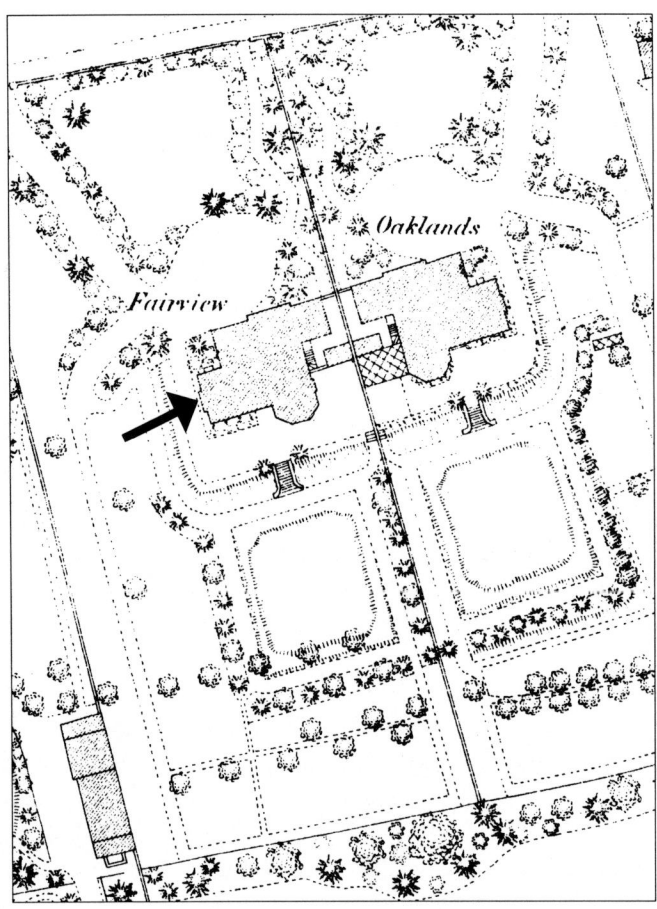

Map showing the site of Fairview House, Cliftonville, 1885 (arrowed)
Courtesy of the Local History Studies, Northampton Central Public Library

...Mr. Abraham Farrar ... has successfully passed the matriculation examination at the London University. As many of our readers are aware, this examination is a very severe one, and includes eleven subjects (Greek, Latin, French and the higher branches of mathematics, natural philosophy and chemistry, etc.)... In the examination he was represented by a number, and favouritism being, therefore, an impossibility, his unique success is the more remarkable.

What an astonishing achievement for Farrar. He said "*Mr. Arnold wished me to proceed for the B.A. degree, but as it meant two years' preparation and as my father preferred a professional career to give me worldly experience, I was instead articled for four years to the leading firm of architects and surveyors at Northampton, continuing to live with Mr. Arnold as a paying guest.*" So he stayed as a boarder at Fairview House for four years, securing an apprenticeship with the firm of architects, Law and Co. in Abington Street. Thus ended the 13 years of the most famous master-pupil relationship in the history of British deaf education. Arnold truly touched Farrar's life for ever.

Farrar's assessment of Mr. Arnold's teaching qualities is worth mentioning:-

Mr. Arnold united a quick sympathy and enthusiasm, to which the dullest scholar yielded. Patient, full of resource and ready to adapt himself to the varying needs and peculiarities of his scholars, he possessed the faculty of engaging their attention and driving a lesson straight home at the right moment, while his strong sense of humour always served to maintain an entente cordiale. At work with them, he was in his element, and his idiosyncrasies showed to the best advantage.

Accustomed to be independent and untrammelled in all he did, he would most probably only have chafed under the shackles of an Institution with its rules and prescribed routine.

Arnold's class continued to be taught along the same oral scheme which he adopted for Farrar. During that time, the public advocacy on the oral method of teaching the deaf gathered momentum everywhere, not only in England, but in European countries too. The British party, including Arnold, attended in Milan in 1880 an international congress, at which delegates represented countries known to have schools for the deaf. Briefly the strongly oral-biased delegates put forward their main resolution, which was passed, and it read:-

The Congress, considering the incontestable superiority of speech over signs in restoring the deaf mute to society, and in giving him a more perfect knowledge of language, declares that the oral method ought to be preferred to that of signs for the education and instruction of the deaf and dumb.

Then another resolution, which was also adopted, was that *the pure oral method should be preferred considering that the simultaneous use of speech and signs has the disadvantage of injuring speech, lipreading and precision of ideas.*

Thus Arnold returned to Northampton feeling elated with the results of the Milan Congress.

From the Northampton census of 1881, the listed deaf boarding pupils in his class were:-

Arthur Levitt (8) from Leeds, Thomas Willett (8) from Norfolk, and William A. Cockayne (16) from Sheffield, and Vivian Watney (10) from London, all born deaf and dumb, and Mary Hardcastle (6) from Newcastle, deaf from scarlet fever at the age of 1 year.

Farrar said in 1934 that:-

All the time I was at school I knew fingerspelling, but it was never used in school by teacher and pupils. I often used it out of school with my fellow-pupils, some of whom had acquired it at other schools before coming to Arnold's. We were strictly told to use fingerspelling, not signs, if we could not always lipread one another's speech – or had the patience to do so – but, as might be expected, it inevitably involved some signing as well... My experience, however, is that very few hearing people know finger-spelling, and I usually ask them to write when I am not always able to read their lips.

Indeed one of Arnold's pupils, William Cockayne, was taught at the YIDD before he came to Northampton and he would be one of Farrar's fellow-pupils who used signs and fingerspelling.

As it is not the object of this book to discuss in detail the teaching methods used by Arnold, references on them can be found in the bibliography. Although Arnold strongly believed in the oral method, he never condemned the manual method, which, he thought, was an inferior method in terms of educational progress. However, he questioned the value of the combined system and did not see any merit in it. Farrar remarked that

...while recognising that the natural signs used by the deaf cannot wholly be dispensed with at the initial stage, Arnold ordinarily refrained from signs and in case of difficulty resorted to the blackboard.

In March 1881, at a Conference of the Governing Bodies of Institutions for the Education of the Deaf held in London, some headmasters showed some reservations about the resolutions passed at the Milan Congress and Arnold was challenged on whether he thought signs were necessary in the period of elementary instruction. His reply was:

Permit a child to express by a sign what he has not a word to express

and emphasised that, in his oral method of teaching, signs were not taught. In his book *"Education of Deaf-Mutes: a Manual for Teachers"* published in 1888, the following extracts seemed to show his support for the use of signs:-

There are serviceable forms of facial expression common to most deaf-mute children which might well be utilised in preparing for speech.

Natural signs have a strong claim to recognition in the education of deaf-mutes...

There is a still greater inducement to employ this realistic method, for it is in the line of the signs in which deaf-mutes delight, but free from their linguistic abuses. Of signs, motion and action, so congenial to and eagerly sought by the young, are the chief elements. Now, both can be enlisted in teaching language, but instead of associating mimic gestures with them we associate their names.

Walter S. Bessant

Arnold secured the services of Mr. Walter S. Bessant, an experienced teacher of the deaf, in 1880 during his school hours. Mr. Bessant and his family moved from his private establishment for deaf boys at Headington, Oxford, to 11 Alfred St., Northampton, bringing with him his private deaf pupil, Alexander E. Miller aged 18 years. He continued to teach Miller, who also received extra tuition from Arnold. Mr. Bessant was instrumental in helping Arnold to complete *A Method of Teaching the Deaf and Dumb Speech, Lipreading and Language*, which was published a year later. This was a guide book for parents of deaf children. In the said book Arnold's class was referred to as the

MIDDLE CLASS SCHOOL FOR THE DEAF AND DUMB

At the end of 1882 Mr. Bessant left to take up his appointment as head of the Oral Department at the Old Trafford Schools, Manchester. In January 1883 Hugh Neville Dixon took his place and received teacher training from Arnold in the next two years.

Farrar thought:-

... as a teacher, Arnold was successful in an exceptional degree not only in speech and lipreading, but in imparting in an incisive manner knowledge to his pupils, even the backward ones, and interesting them in their lessons, especially in history.

One of Arnold's less able pupils was Mary Hardcastle, who came to Northampton at the age of six years in 1881. She had been with Arnold for five years and was next transferred to Ealing College for two years. Then she was transferred to the YIDD, Doncaster, as a private pupil of the headmaster, Mr. James Howard, who remarked that Mary came to Doncaster in 1888 *with very little power of speech, a most unnatural voice and very small vocabulary*. After six years at Doncaster, Mary returned to Newcastle. Her father, Nicholas Hardcastle, who was a well-known surgeon, asserted that Mary owed her education to Doncaster. As every pioneer has his or her own successes and failures, Arnold later claimed that most of his deaf pupils were taught speech with success except the one who had a cleft palate. This deaf pupil, with whom Arnold did not succeed, happened to be Mary Hardcastle.

James Howard's notes on Mary Hardcastle
Courtesy of Doncaster Archives (ref. SR 90/9/7)

Arnold's school never had more than nine pupils at a time and he taught a total of about 20 pupils from 1874 to 1884.

The Rev. Thomas Arnold retired from teaching at the end of December 1884. At the same time Farrar successfully completed his apprenticeship with the architectural company, qualified as a surveyor and architect and left for Leeds. He never practised the profession but, instead, being a man of means, he focussed on his hobby, geology, and later received the Fellowship of the Geological Society in 1887 for his research work and findings on the cliffs of Cromer.

A survey of all schools of the deaf in the United Kingdom, published in 1884, revealed the following information:-

Oral School for the Deaf, est. 1860, Fairview, Cliftonville, Northampton. 9 pupils and 2 teachers.

Was the school established in either 1860 or 1868? No answer can be given but the general consensus is that the official year of its establishment is 1868.

The Rev. Thomas Arnold conversing with his three female students

The Arnold Way

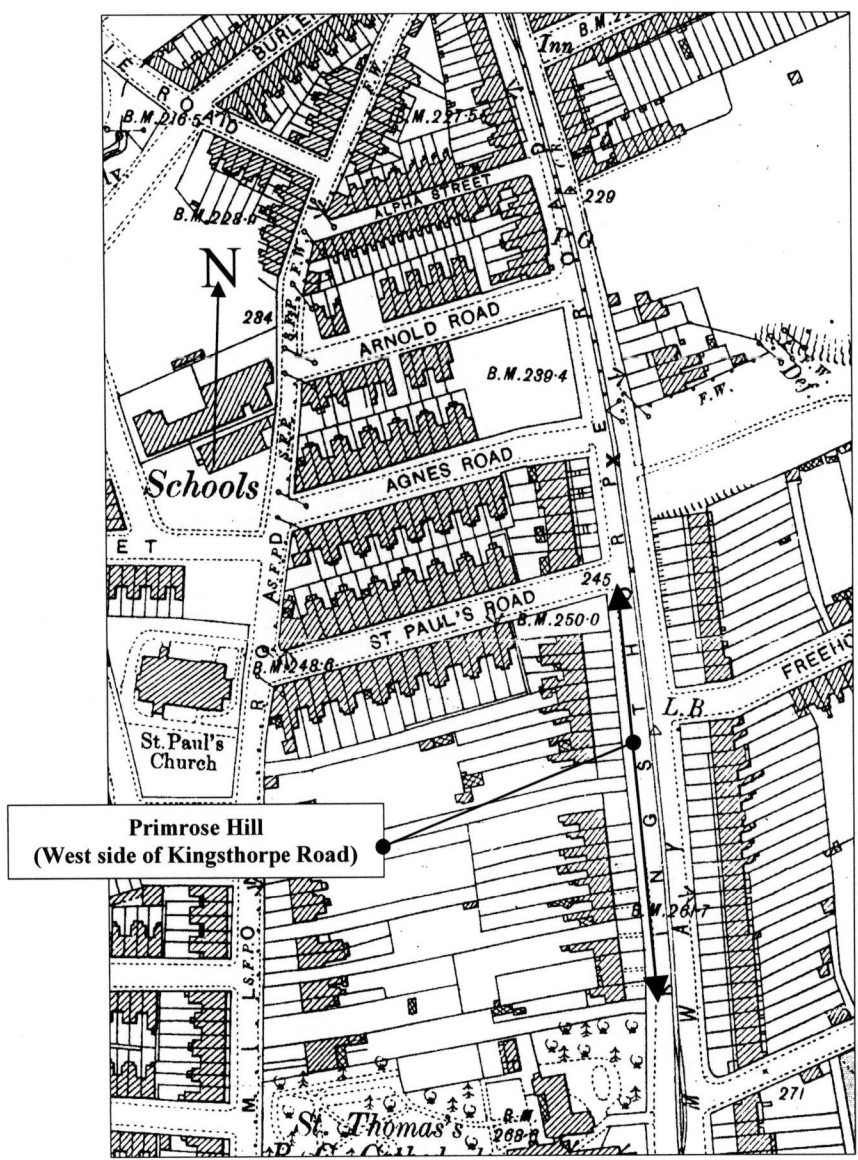

Map showing the sites of Primrose Hill and St. Paul's Road, 1901
(Note Arnold Road, named after the Rev. Thomas Arnold after his death in 1897)

Courtesy of Local History Studies, Northampton Central Public Library.

Chapter 2

The Dixon Era (1885 – 1908)

In 1883 Hugh Neville Dixon, a brilliant academician, joined Arnold as an assistant teacher. After 68 years old Arnold's resignation, Mr. Dixon took over on January 1st 1885. The tenancy of Fairview House ceased and he took the newly built premises at 25 St. Paul's Road for his class of deaf boys. Arnold lived next door at no. 27 and carried on educating at least two of his female deaf students, namely Mary Hardcastle (11), and Christine Wilson (10), who eventually became his adopted daughter.

25 & 27 St. Paul's Road, Northampton, 2008

Dixon came from a well-off farming family and received education at Witham, Essex, and Southgate, Middlesex. He obtained B.A. and M.A. degrees from London University as well as his M.A. in Classics in 1883 at Christ's College, Cambridge, all with first class honours. Whilst at Cambridge, he was encouraged to take an in-depth study of botany by Professor Babbington and from this his lifelong study of mosses grew. He was a Fellow and one-time Vice-President of the Linnaean Society and became the world's foremost authority on mosses. He produced a classic guidebook on mosses for students. During the summer vacations, he often went out fell walking in the English Lake District and was a fast walker over long distances. He was a remarkable man with many sporting interests. He played hockey up to the age of 50 years and was an ice-skater, who skated from Northampton to Peterborough with Hudson the Amateur Skating Champion despite falling through the ice three times! Such was Mr. Dixon, an all-round and energetic sportsman. Apart from this, he was quiet and unassuming and showed kindness and was approachable. Whilst in Northampton, Dixon met a local lady, Mary Pressland, who helped him as house mother to the boys and who also did some teaching, and on December 22 1887 they were married. Their only son, Neville, died tragically at the age of 7 in 1900.

Hugh N. Dixon, M.A., F.L.S.

In 1889 Dixon's class of deaf boys moved to a newly built three-storied house at 23 East Park Parade, Northampton, on the road to Kettering. The house was named *Wickham House* as Mr. Dixon's ancestors came from Wickham in Essex. There was a brass plate outside the entrance door and the title read *Oral School for the Deaf*. Due to its limited room-space, the number of deaf boarders was rarely more than seven.

Wickham House, East Park Parade, Northampton, 2000

Mr. Dixon attended the National Association of Teachers of the Deaf (abbreviated NATD) conferences on deaf education and was one of the three representatives for private schools, the other two being Mr. Barber and Miss Mary Hare. He took a passive role in most meetings but if he heard some statements that he did not agree with, he would speak up. For example: after a talk by van Praagh, a teacher of the deaf from London who believed in pure oralism, Dixon agreed tactfully with what was said, but as he did not believe in lessons based on lipreading only, he said that it was a waste of time lipreading which did not give information. Dixon always gave his class reading lessons and geography lessons with a special view to develop lipreading skills. This was a notable departure from the standard lipreading practice set by Arnold. Apart from that, Arnold's practical method of speech teaching adopted by Dixon continued. The responses, which Mr. Dixon gave in conferences, give us some useful clues as to how he dealt with his class of deaf children at Northampton. Regarding letter-writing, he encouraged children to write letters themselves freely to parents and friends so that they would learn from their corrected letters. He thought it was important for children to express their own ideas. During the 1890s, there were controversial debates on the methods of communication, and every time Mr. Dixon faced a barrage of criticisms from anti-oralists, he invited them to his school to see how his school was being run. He had a beard and he thought that if his pupils could lipread him, then they could lipread anyone!

One of his first pupils in 1885 was the 12 years old Cyril Carr, whose deafness at the age of three was caused by a fever. He had been educated at three different hearing schools in Sheffield with little success. At Northampton, Cyril rapidly made progress and developed his skills in science, specially astronomy and microscopy, and, after leaving school in 1890, he was employed as a laboratory assistant and eventually became a qualified dentist. Another pupil, Henry Francis, was the first of Mr. Dixon's pupils to pass the examinations of the College of Preceptors in 1892 and is worthy of mention because of the wide range of subjects which he took and passed:- English grammar, Scripture and English history,

Cyril Carr

Geography, Arithmetic, Drawing and Geometry. His name was not amongst those listed on the Roll of Honours Board, a surprising omission.

In 1890 Bonet's *Method of Teaching Deaf Mutes to Speak* was published and was the result of Mr. Dixon's translation from the original Spanish. In it was a long historical introduction by Abraham Farrar. It was a classical piece of work by Mr. Dixon.

Alan P. Allsebrook wrote from British Columbia, Canada, in 1932:-

... thirty-eight years have passed since I entered Mr. Dixon's school on East Park Parade... The years steal on, and on.
I was a spindle-legged, tow headed kid of fourteen then, with the nerve and physical grit of an average rabbit, if as much!
What were you doing up the Amazon, George Bottomley? Tut! Tut! You were six, I recall, when I entered Wickham House. Do you recollect the stuffed pussy-cat you used to take to bed with you for protection against – er – bogies? And how we used to make you howl by taking it from you and throwing it from bed to bed? And Don Eady was nine those days.

Mr. Frederick Ince-Jones joined Mr. Dixon as a pupil-teacher in 1901 and, as his special subject was Botany, he could not have asked for a better teacher than Mr. Dixon himself.

He observed Mr. Dixon's way of teaching speech and lipreading and considered him to be a fine teacher of deaf boys. Being a young and inexperienced young man, he was faced with two untaught boys, one of 4 years of age and the other 5 years old. He was allowed to work out the lessons for himself. For the next 14 years the two said boys were in the care of Mr. Ince-Jones, who remarked in later years that some of his methods invited criticism, in which case he would have modified them.

Mr. Dixon's star pupils were:-

Charles Lynton Mallet, the second son of Walter E. Mallet, jeweller and silversmith of Barnstaple, Devon. He was the first pupil to enter university and he studied Chemistry at St. John's College, University of Oxford, from 1903 to 1907, obtaining a B.A. degree. He died at his home in Bath in 1910 at the age of 26.

The second pupil, Charles Gordon Douglas-Irvine, was born deaf in Northampton, the son of Walter Douglas Irvine, a landed proprietor. He had a brother, William, and a sister, Kate, both born deaf. He was admitted at the age of five and received tuition for 11 years. Dixon said Charles had a highly strung temperament, was both impulsive and mentally alert and was easy to teach. Charles was very anxious to learn but easily forgot. His speech and lip-reading were said to be remarkably good. At 13 years of age, he took the examinations at the College of Preceptors and passed them. Subjects taken were Scripture History, English Language, English History, Geography, Arithmetic, Geometry and Drawing. Two years later he took the Cambridge Junior Local examinations, but failed *owing to over excitement*. A few months later his father died and Charles left school. He was placed under Mr. Gimmel in his private laboratory in Edinburgh for 3 months and then had another 4 months' advanced study with a private tutor. By October 1903, at the age of 18 years, he passed the Edinburgh University entrance examinations in Higher Mathematics, Chemistry and the two compulsory subjects, Latin and English, and in September 1904 he obtained *Second Honours* in Chemistry. In those days, to become an analytical chemist, there were two options open to applicants at Edinburgh University, the first leading to a degree and the second demanding longer practical study but making less demand on the abilities to obtain the required qualifications. Charles Irvine took the second option.

Noel G. Maddison

The third pupil, Noel G. Maddison, (later Noel Brunning-Maddison) was born deaf in 1889. His father was a solicitor in the City of London. In 1894 Noel attended 11 Fitzroy Square, London, and was taught by van Praagh for 8 years. After that, he was Mr. Dixon's pupil for three years. To study Chemistry with a view of making it his career, he attended Chemistry lectures and laboratory work at the Northampton Technical School. Although he was unable to follow the lectures, he enjoyed following the blackboard illustrations on experiments. To compensate for his inability to follow the oral lectures, Mr. Ince-Jones gave support by going over with him the notes from one of Noel's colleagues. Then Noel Maddison entered the Royal College of Science, University of London, South Kensington in 1907. He passed examinations in Chemistry, Physics, Mechanics, Geology and Astronomy and became a chemical analyst. Mr. Ince-Jones lectured on Botany at the Northampton Technical College for adults and also gave lessons on the same subject to a class of deaf pupils. His methods for both classes were not very different. He wrote:-

To the deaf "listeners" I spoke more slowly, chose my words more carefully because they would not lipread those which they did not know, and used the blackboard rather more freely for putting up some new scientific expressions calling for more explanations than were necessary for hearing students, but on the whole the progress of the deaf was not much slower. The reason was that the deaf boys were familiar with my speech and my articulation was clear.

Noel G. Maddison working in the laboratory

It is a pity that Mr. Dixon took a passive role in NATD conferences and that he did not deliver any major paper to summarise the achievements of his ex-pupils during his spell at Wickham House, perhaps out of modesty, but at least he showed in practice that deaf children could be taught to the level of university education. That was his legacy.

Mr. Dixon attended his last NATD meeting in London in 1908 and towards the end of the meeting,

Mr. Dixon being obliged to leave for a train asked for permission to notify members that at the Pinafore Factory at Northampton deaf girls will be able to obtain good employment and the foreman is willing to receive such.

What an amazing gesture of goodwill and farewell!

Mr. Dixon and his wife, Mary, ended their teaching careers after 23 years at the end of the year 1908. On June 11 1910 a presentation to Mr and Mrs Dixon took place at Wickham House, East Park Parade, and they received a silver tea service as a token of appreciation from former pupils. Among the old boys attending were Charles H. B. Condy, Donald C. Eady, Noel Maddison, Cyril Carr and Alan Allsebrook.

Alan Allsebrook gave a speech :-

You ask me for a few words on behalf of the Old Boys of Wickham House. It is almost superfluous on my part to say how honoured I feel, and how much pleasure it is to me, as to us all, to see once again the faces of schoolfellows and friends of boyhood's days. To you, in particular, Mr and Mrs Dixon, on behalf of your old pupils, I would tender our grateful tribute of thanks and affectionate appreciation for all you did for us in equipping us for our fight through the world.

Alan Allsebrook

Boys, I now realise, are very embryo animals. I doubt if we appreciated properly, in the old days, your care and thought for us. These things are only found out when one's hobbledehoy years are passed. It is then that we realise the great truth, that when we leave school, with all its restraints, rules and disciplines, we enter – NOT freedom! – but a larger and sterner school – the school of life and the world. And we soon find out that the discipline there is harder, and the punishments for our breaches of the world's discipline much more severe and lasting, and we must all go on learning our lessons year after year.

It is on this account that we thank you, Mr. and Mrs. Dixon, for your excellent training. We thank you especially for your earnest endeavours – as far as our wills would carry us – to make us honest English gentlemen and real men. Speaking for myself, I can vividly remember that I had a strong leaning towards cotton-wool in those days. I can thank you now, that you saw to it that we had none of that, though your care and thoughtfulness for our physical well-being never left anything to be desired. We all unite in wishing you many years of happy leisure and health after your long course of labours

This speech was followed up by the presentation to the Dixon couple of a letter filled with signatures of ex-pupils to the Dixon couple. Henceforth Mr. Dixon carried out a life-time research on mosses, but showed interest in his old pupils' progress now and then.

The Arnold Way

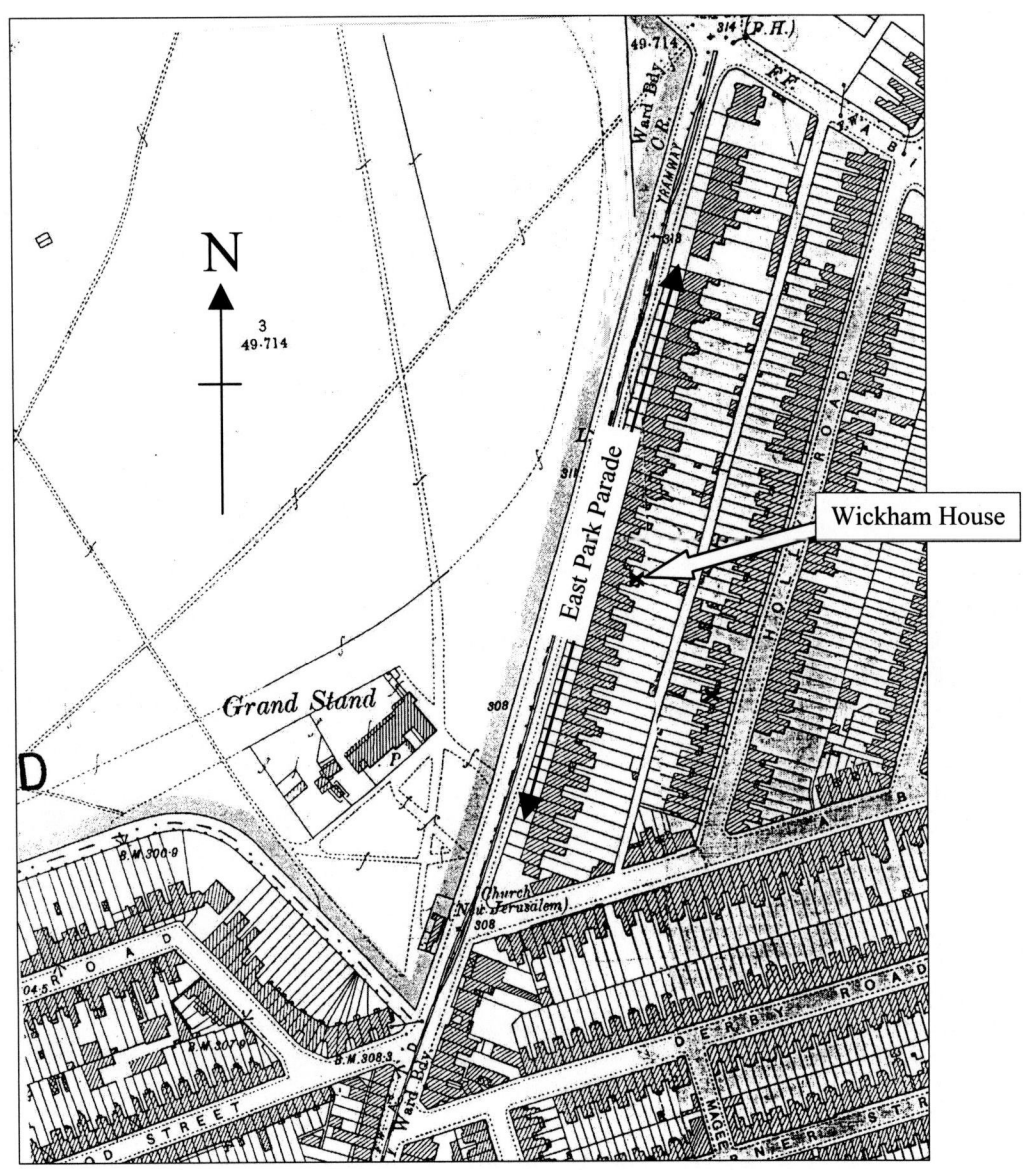

Map showing the site of Wickham House, East Park Parade, 1901

Courtesy of Local History Studies, Northampton Central Public Library.

Chapter 3

The Ince-Jones Era (1909 - 1929)

Frederick Ince-Jones was born in Islington, London, on May 12 1883, the eldest son of the Rev. Frederick A. Jones, who was a Baptist Minister. The name Ince came from his paternal grandmother. He was educated at the City of London School and, at the age of 17 years, he resided at 1 York Road near Cliftonville, Northampton, and was trained by Mr. Dixon for three years before becoming a qualified teacher of the deaf in March 1904. For the next five years he was a teacher of Botany at the Northampton and County Technical and Art Schools, Abington Square. In 1907 he obtained his B.Sc. honours degree at London University and finally he was called to the Bar at the Inner Temple, London, but did not pursue a career in law.

The fact that Mr. Ince-Jones gave his tutorial support to Noel Maddison's chemistry lessons with much success probably led him to believe that he had the talent to raise the educational standards of the deaf to a higher level. He joined the membership of the NATD in 1904 and four years later, he was voted into the Executive Committee of the NATD. This is remarkable when it is considered that most of its members were highly experienced teachers of the deaf of long standing.

In 1906 he joined Mr. Dixon as a partner, knowing that Mr. Dixon would step down in two years' time. When the day of reckoning arrived, Mr. Ince-Jones became the third head of the High School for the Oral Education of the Deaf in January 1909. He was aware that there was no special provision whatever for the education of a secondary type for the brighter and more intelligent deaf children. He saw an opportunity of developing his school into a private secondary school for deaf boys and at the same time running a preparatory class for young entrants and gearing them to the secondary level of education.

Wickham House was still being used as the School site, but on a temporary basis. On the domestic side, the post of Matron went to Miss E.M.M. Phillips, a qualified teacher of the deaf, having been trained at the Ealing Training College of Teachers of the Deaf. The next two years saw Mr. Ince-Jones looking around for a suitable premises in order to expand his school.

It was in 1911 that Spring Hill House and its premises of one acre in Cliftonville, Northampton, were vacant. Spring Hill House was probably built during the early 1850s as there were other newly-built large mansions appearing at the same time in the Cliftonville area. *(See Note 9)* The House was mainly a residential house and did not need much alteration. After Mr. Ince-Jones's purchase of the premises, the brick stable and the coach house were converted into a schoolroom and a workshop respectively. The front of the house with its porch was clad with wisteria. It was announced in *The Teacher of the Deaf* (December 1912 issue) that:-

The High School for the Deaf at Northampton has removed from East Park Parade to a larger and better premises at Spring Hill, Cliftonville, Northampton. Those who remember the school in the time of the late Rev. Thomas Arnold will be interested to learn that Spring Hill is only a stone's throw from the house [Fairview House] occupied by him at the time of his retirement.

The Arnold Way

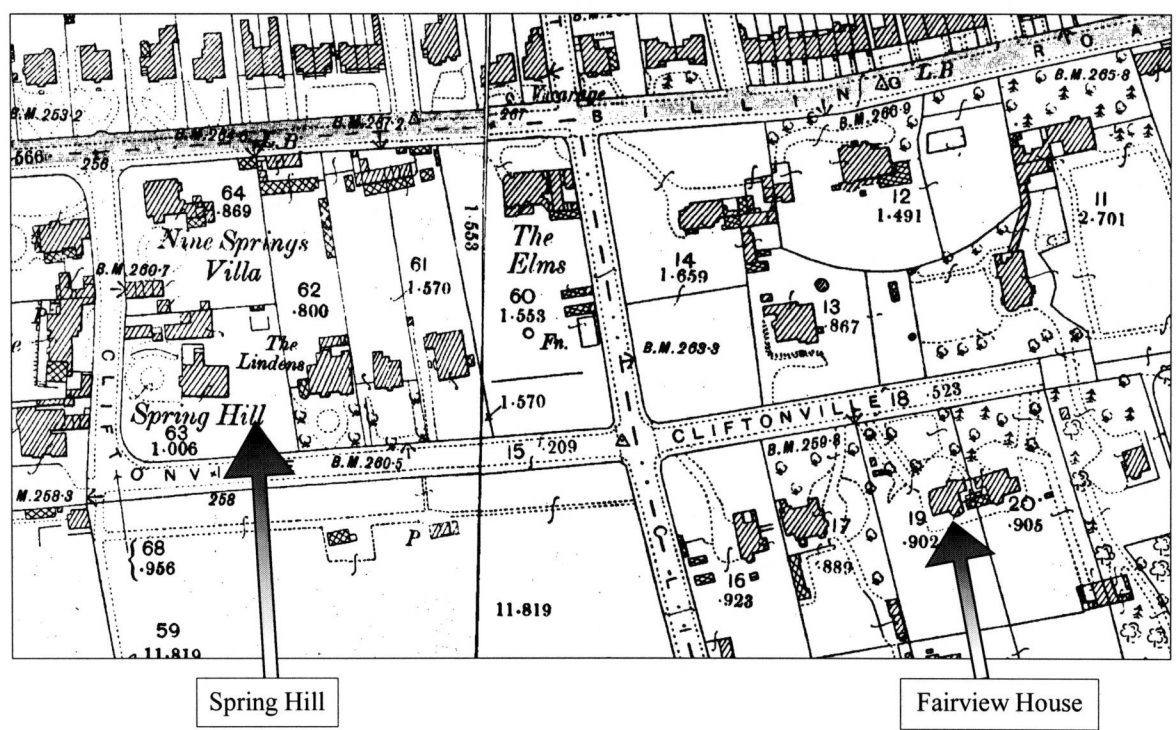

Map of Cliftonville, Northampton (1901)
Courtesy of Local History Studies, Northampton Central Public Library

Mr. Ince-Jones prepared his school curriculum and his school prospectus was then distributed to the public at large.

Frederick William Illingworth, aged 20, the youngest son of Mr. F. B. Illingworth (the late headmaster of the Liverpool School for the Deaf) was Mr. Ince-Jones's first teacher-trainee employed at Spring Hill. Mr. Illingworth had some years' teaching experience at the Glasgow Institution for the Deaf. His prowess in the cricket field made him a favourite of the boys. However, on the outbreak of the First World War he was called up at once. Mr. Horace Haycock replaced him, but 18 months later he was called up. While Mr. Ince-Jones was looking for teachers who had some experience of teaching the deaf, two part-time local teachers were recruited to help out. It was not long before Miss C. King, a teacher of the deaf from Margate School for the Deaf, joined the staff.

On June 7 1917 Fl. Lieut. Illingworth of the Scottish Rifles, who had been attached to the Royal Air Force, was shot down during a battle in France and was wounded in the lung. He was taken as a prisoner of war to Holzminde Camp. Whilst there, he gained a reputation for his daring attempts to escape by tunnelling his way out. After the war he was still weak and spent his remaining years with his family at Joppa, Edinburgh. He died at his home on February 6 1919 at the age of 27 and was interred in Portobello Cemetery on February 9 *with full military honours*. Fl. Lieut. H. Haycock was awarded the Military Cross and joined the teaching staff at Margate School for the Deaf after completing his war service with the R.A.F. in 1921.

The accommodation at Spring Hill House was sufficient for 21 boys and residential staff. It started with 14 boys during the First World War and it was in the 1920s when the house was finally booked full.

Boys were admitted at any age after 5 years, and 11 or 12 years was an average age on entry. There was no entrance examination. Few of them came from ordinary deaf schools, some from other private schools for the deaf, and some from homes where early private tuition was received. They were mostly sons of socially well-to-do parents, who were able to afford the high fees charged by Mr. Ince-Jones for their education. Few left before the age of 18 and many stayed longer to obtain qualifications by examination. Thus there was no limit of age at which the boys had to leave. Their parents were usually persuaded to allow their sons to remain until Mr. Ince-Jones thought he had done all he could for them.

Alexander Bilibin

Alexander Bilibin (1913 – 1925) at the age of nine recovered from an operation behind his ears to prevent total loss of sight, but this resulted him becoming totally deaf. His father, Sergei, was a Russian freelance artist and travelled to European cities to earn his commissions. The Bilibin family came to London and settled there. Alexander and his father went to Northampton after receiving information that there was a school there that claimed a good rate of success in teaching deaf children speech and lipreading. Mr. Ince-Jones showed them round the school and allowed them to see his pupils. Alexander knew no word of English, but Mr. Ince-Jones gave an assurance that Alexander would be able to speak good English after a year or two. Early in 1913 the ten year-old Alexander entered the *Ince-Jones Oral School*. True to Mr. Ince-Jones's word, Alexander spoke English well and worked hard to improve his grammar. In Arthur F. Dimmock's *Tommy*, his interview with Alexander Bilibin, who reminisced on his days at Northampton, revealed the following information:-

Miss Shackleton (matron) and Miss C. King with boys (circa 1917)

Garden Plot

At the school, sign language was banned although some pupils used it on the sly. Caning was the penalty for those who got caught. Alexander had a strong disinclination to sign. This put him high in the regard of Mr. Ince-Jones although his torrid temper sometimes earned him black looks from the head and staff. The school was a fee-paying boys only concern. Sergei and Anita (Alexander's parents) made periodical visits to see how their son was getting on and to pay the fees which were by monthly instalments, a special arrangement between Sergei and the head. Alexander's progress in speech pleased the couple. The school provided tuition in art. This was where Alexander excelled alongside a younger boy called Skuse.

Alexander's Art tutor was Mr. James Wilson Baxter, who held the qualifications of A.R.C.A., Royal College of Art, South Kensington, and was an Art master at Northampton Town and County School (re-named Northampton Grammar School for Boys in 1946). He was the longest serving part-time teacher at Spring Hill.

Lyonel Pritchard

Lyonel Pritchard (1917 – 1930), who stayed for 14 years, gave the earliest description of the layout of the rooms of Spring Hill House:-

I remember the Residential House which was dominated by a huge porch where the boys were welcomed back every term. Two large windows were blocked up during the time of the Window Tax and stared out blindly. A long corridor ran from the porch straight to the dining room which was heavily panelled in oak with a large open fireplace; in the dining room were two tables, one of them convertible for billiards and there was a parquet floor. To the right of the dining room led off to the Principal's Office and his private lounge, to the left were a library, staircase, kitchen and food stores.

On the first floor were the eight bedrooms and dormitories, Mr. Ince-Jones' suite, Matron's next to the sick bay and Residential Teacher's near the junior dormitory. There were four bedrooms for the pupils, five beds in one for the smallest juniors, four beds in the next junior room; the middle and senior bedrooms had six occupants each.

The Dining Room

Spring Hill Lawn (1910s)

The Big Schoolroom (1920s)

Oliver Cayley (1917 – 1925) entered Spring Hill School in May 1917 and recalled his early days during the First World War:-

AN EXCITING NIGHT AT SPRING HILL IN 1917.

J. Oliver Cayley

On the night of October 19th 1917, five of us, Gordon Calder, Cyril France, Eric Gourlay, the late Roger Thorman and myself were sound asleep in the middle dormitory. It was my second term and I was only eleven years old.

Suddenly Mr. Ince-Jones burst into our peaceful bedroom, shaking me first (my bed was near the door) and then the other boys. I did wake up but fell asleep again at once! Later I was told that Mr. Ince-Jones seized my bed clothes, flung them over the end of my bed, picked me up and shoved me out of the room with my clothes or dressing-gown following me. I was left outside half-awake and bewildered. While I was being bundled out of the bedroom, I had a momentary glimpse of Gordon Calder, the master of our bedroom, standing in his long night-gown beside his bed and staring open-mouthed!

The boys all came out of the room but not so quickly as I did! George Goodwin, the eldest boy in the school, coming out of his small bedroom above the front door, met us at the top of the stairs. Then we were ordered to go down the cellar at once! To the cellar! And I began to think we were going to be punished for some very naughty deed. What it was, I had no idea. As soon as we started to descend the stairs, I saw Mr. Ince-Jones rush into the corridor.

To our surprise we found in the cellar the late Miss Shackleton (our matron), Miss King (our mistress), the old cook whose face was very white with fear, two servants and four little boys, Bobby Byers, with a tuft of hair standing upright on one side of his forehead, Percy Molyneux, Lyonel Pritchard and his brother Kenneth, a new boy aged five.

A few moments later six big boys, Arnold Banks, Vivian Yorke, Freddie Kinloch, Serge Cheremeteff, the late Richard Nolan, and Andy Charlton, joined us. Last of all came Mr. Ince-Jones himself. In the cellar were twenty two people, including sixteen boys.

We waited there for sometime, and we little boys were wondering what it was all about. Lyonel, aged eight, asked Mr. Ince-Jones "What for?" Unfortunately I do not remember how he was answered. Mr. Ince-Jones went mysteriously up and down the stairs from time to time during our long wait which, I believe, must have lasted an hour or more. It seemed to us little boys such a long time to wait.

At last all of us went back to bed but we, little boys, were still mystified.

The next morning before breakfast, the secret was out. We saw in the Daily Mirror that there had been an air-raid carried out by the German Zeppelins over the Midlands. The Zeppelins lost their way but dropped bombs in the fog below. One bomb wrecked a house near Northampton Castle Station and three other bombs fell into a field close to the iron-ore quarries worked between Danes' Camp and the blast furnaces. We went there a few days later and found three big holes in the field close to the road and not far from the entrance to the railway tunnel.

Oliver Cayley also gave an account of some comical behaviour of new entrants at Spring Hill:-

You know there is not usually anything funny connected with the departure of a boy from the School for the last time, but some of the new boys are often comical during their first hours at the School.

I think George Talmadge celebrated his first night at school by spilling a jugful of water in his dormitory. He ended his schooldays by spilling a jugful of water in the bathroom much to the headmaster's annoyance.

I, myself, arrived in the big schoolroom one day late, to find the boys doing their afternoon lessons when the masters were out. Serge Cheremeteff hammered his big desk with his fist to attract my attention, then pointed excitedly at the nearest boy at the end of a long row of desks and said, "You see that new boy? His name is Fred Smallman", and then grinned at him. I thought it was a funny name. Fred shook his finger – rather a feminine gesture – at Serge!

Bryan Taylor, aged five, was the most affectionate new boy I had ever seen, particularly towards the members of the Staff. I remember seeing him in the garden putting his arms round Mr. Ince-Jones' leg, thus preventing him from moving forward while gazing at him affectionately!

Fergus Peacocke and Wynne Coates who arrived from Ireland at the same time, started almost directly they entered the big schoolroom to out-talk some of us. Wynne bared his arm and asked us to feel his biceps. Someone then asked Fergus and Wynne to give a boxing display and they did. Wynne put up his fists in front of him with the palm of his hands facing his opponent, a quaint attitude that delighted Alexander Bilibin who slapped his thigh for joy.

Harry Shwer from South Africa, stood on the fender with his back to the big schoolroom fire above which hung a large map. He was showing off before the boys and gave the lapels of his coat a tug. Instantly the map of the great and glorious British Isles crashed on the South African's head, covering him like a tea-cosy. Nothing of South Africa remained visible except trouser legs and shoes. Unfortunately I did not witness this incident but Serge gave a dramatic reproduction of it for my benefit.

And now for Tom McClure. While we were unpacking, Tom showed us in his trunk a beautiful home-made cake complete with knife. He was about to cut it when I intervened, telling him that it was not allowed in the bedroom but only downstairs.
"Why?" said Tom.
"Because it is against the rules of the School."
"Why?"
"Mr. Ince-Jones does not allow it."
"Why?"
I was completely at a loss for an answer. What would you have said?

Lyonel Pritchard continued:-

I was the first boy under 10 years to enter the school – at the early age of six, and I have clear memories of what I suffered amongst those many older and bigger boys. Fortunately three more young pupils also came at the end of my first year in school. Generally, though, the pupils started late and some were from overseas – from U.S.A., Spain, Turkey or South America. Some English pupils came from private schools, for example, Miss Mary Hare's Dene Hollow School at Burgess Hill, (see Note 2), Miss Taylor's School at Hatch End, or Miss Bullock's at Reading.

Mr. Ince-Jones sometimes had to face frantic parents who were willing to pay high fees

Lawn Tennis Court

Group of boys, circa 1922
Back: Fred Smallman, Jack Gibbons, Eric Gourley, George Talmadge, Wilfred _____
Next: Wynne Coates, Oliver Cayley, Eric Hodges, Reggie Sawdon, Robert Byers, Tom McClure, Lyonel Pritchard, Dick. Young
Kneeling: Donald Denison, Jack Attwood, Fergus Peacock
Sitting: Jimmy England, Raymond Thorpe, Kenneth Pritchard, Freddy Davey

The Arnold Way

View of Cliftonville Road from Billing Road, circa 1930
Courtesy of P. Gibbons

The entrance to Spring Hill

The Stables

The entrance to the Stables

Entrance to Spring Hill from Cliftonville Road (2008)

Mr. Ince-Jones's car Morris Cowley, 1929
Courtesy of P. Gibbons

for the education of their backward children. But it was quite exceptional to allow such pupils in the school – if they did enter school under certain circumstances then they often stayed in the same group for a long time and kept back the better pupils.

In their first week at school the new boys were always tested thoroughly in talent-writing and answers to questions before being placed in Forms. There was never any question of considering the boys' ages before placing them in Forms as in other schools.

Kenneth Pritchard (1917 – 1932), another Springhillian of more than 14 years, was the younger brother of Lyonel Pritchard and noted down some changes which he saw during the early 1920s :-

Kenneth Pritchard

The first change I remember was the disappearance of the tall cedar tree which was a little higher than the house and stood on the lawn at the western end of the tennis court near the study. Some of us were disappointed when it went, for we used to climb it! On the other hand it was a great improvement to our tennis lawn for it gave us more space; and some boys, like Lyonel, welcomed it because they would no longer have to search its branches for lost balls. A round holly bush on the southern side of the lawn was removed for similar reasons. When new grass had grown on the bare spots, we were able to have a putting lawn as well as a tennis court.

In 1923 Mr. Ince-Jones bought a Morris-Cowley car so one of the three stables was converted into a garage. The first accommodated our bicycles, the second the car and the third Dandy, Miss Knowles' dog. She was the lady teacher then. As bicycles grew in number the third stable was used to house some of them and Miss Knowles bought a big kennel which was kept near the workshop.

The teaching accommodation comprised two rooms, *the small Schoolroom* for the Junior form and *the big Schoolroom,* which was forty feet long and partitioned into two by screens for the Senior and the Middle forms. The Senior form usually consisted of six boys and the Middle form another six boys.

Mr. Baxter came to assist "on loan" for a few hours every Thursday afternoon. Additional tutorials were also given by teacher-trainees from Manchester University. After the 1st World War, Mr. Ince-Jones decided to get someone young to absorb and carry on his teaching methods. He thought that the earlier a teacher became familiar with the problems of the deaf, the better he would succeed. So he chose a boy of just 16 years of age, Edgar Lewis Mundin. At first, naturally, Mr. Mundin was not involved in the teaching for he was younger than many of the pupils, but he gradually adapted himself well. Besides his training, he was given time and opportunity to continue his advanced studies. For drill and physical training, a sergeant major from the Northampton regiment was employed until Mr. Mundin took over in 1920. Both Mr. Ince-Jones and Mr. Mundin were the main teachers for the Senior and Middle forms from 1920 to 1943 and the School timetable and routine did not vary much throughout.

Mr. Mundin was born in Northampton on August 23rd 1904 and was educated at Northampton Grammar School and London University, at which he graduated with a B.A. degree, with Honours in Geography in 1927; his Secondary Teachers' Diploma a year later and the NCTD

Edgar Lewis Mundin

Diploma in 1929 with Honours in History, Speech, Anatomy and Practical Teaching. The description of Mr. Mundin was *"Slight, very dark, very neat, almost dapper, he radiated a kind of spare efficiency - all his movements were rapid, frugal but precise."* He taught History and Geography and was in charge of games. He also took the Senior class for Carpentry. Some of his pupils turned into skilled carpenters, particularly Christopher Ham who became a professional wood carver. At that time Mr. Mundin had been living with his father, Mr. Edgar Porch Mundin, who was a well known local cabinet maker and the founder of the Mundin Brothers furnishing firm in Abington Street. From his father Mr. E. L. Mundin inherited a peculiarly reverential attitude to tools and craftsmanship, an appreciation of the grain and quality of good wood and well-made furniture.

Lyonel Pritchard described the School timetable and routine taken at Spring Hill:-

<u>Daily School Timetable.</u>

7. 45	Arise (Sunday 8.15)
8.15 - 8.45	Breakfast.
8.45 - 9.15	Newspaper reading.
9.15 - 9.45	"News of the Term" followed by speech work. This was a special lesson expressed orally and it often led to exchange of opinions and even arguments. Current school news, politics, and daily news from all over the world were taught and analysed from different viewpoints. Some general reading from newspapers was included for the benefit of speech development and lipreading practice. Immediately after the news period, the previous night's homework was marked and corrected. Oral questions and answers were also given. For slower pupils, or those who had neglected their work, the failure in oral question- and- answer meant completing the exercise standing up during the dinner hour. Mental arithmetic often caused us to think rapidly and it was always speed and accuracy that the teachers demanded.
9.45 - 10.45	Classwork on Arithmetic and Mathematics, Geometry, Algebra, Applied Mathematics, Trigonometry, Higher Maths as well as training in Book Keeping and mapwork practice. The level of work was entirely dependent on the pupil's abilities.
10.45 – 11.00	Break for milk. Sometimes minor medical check-up.
11.00 – 12.30	Varied programme of work in Religious Knowledge, Geography, Shakespeare, Botany, Practical Chemistry or English Composition.
12.30 – 1.00	In summer, swimming practice on Tuesday and Friday. In winter, drill. Monday, Tuesday and Thursday was free pupil time.
1pm – 2pm	Lunch break
2.00 – 3.00	On days except Wednesday, English History, French or Art. Wednesday p.m. was half day off for Seniors while Juniors did woodwork or football practice.
3.00 – 5.00	Games period (football, cricket, cross country runs). Gardening.
5.00 – 5.30	Tea
5.30 – 5.50	Break
5.50 – 7.20	Preparation work. Speech work by Mr. Ince-Jones.
7.20 – 7.40	Supper.

The weekend programme was typical of a residential school; Saturday meant letters home and free time for shopping in town. Sometimes in the morning there was Junior drill. In the afternoon, Seniors did woodwork for two hours while Juniors had a free afternoon for walks. Saturday evenings were free for leisure time.

Sunday morning service was at 11am in the All Saints Parish Church. Winter afternoons were for walks, summer afternoons were allowed for relaxation. In the winter evenings from 5 to 7 pm there was evening Sunday school with Bible reading and Prayer book study supervised by Mr. Ince-Jones.

Kenneth Pritchard recalled:-

In April 1923 to our surprise and delight Mr. Ince-Jones was married; and when Patricia was born in 1925, the tuck room in the north-eastern corner of the house was converted into a delightful nursery for Patricia and Pamela who came two years later. After the change we kept our tuck in big, new cupboards in the passage.

Strolling in the countryside
Mr. & Mrs. Ince-Jones with Miss Lawrence and Mr. Mundin
Courtesy of Philip Gibbons

Mr. F. Ince-Jones's marriage to Miss Sarah Elizabeth Keown, who was born in Crouch End in 1895, took place at Highgate, London, and the local newspaper had almost one page devoted to the descriptive listing of wedding presents received. Mrs. Ince-Jones took over the responsibility of supervising the domestic side of the School.

Stanley G. Powell (1926 – 1930), the son of working class parents, became totally deaf at the age of seven years. He attended the day school in Bristol under Miss Virgo, who, struck by his abilities, was instrumental in raising funds and grants to enable Stanley to go to Northampton. In his article from *The Volta Bureau* (April 1943) on Mr. Ince-Jones's School for

Stanley G. Powell

Deaf Boys, Stanley wrote about the development of the boys' character, a point to which Mr. Ince-Jones attached great importance:-

... He [Mr. Ince-Jones] rightly regards mental development without the backing of a sound character as useless. There were, in my time, three or four boys known as prefects to whom was delegated the responsibility of maintaining discipline and order at times when the teaching staff were not present. These boys were chosen for their inherent qualities as leaders – and were not always the eldest or most advanced or physically the strongest pupils. This system ... subconsciously educates the boys in their responsibilities, duties and behaviour towards those in authority and those under them. Far more useful in the development of character and an appreciation of the issues of life is Mr. Ince-Jones' method of studying the Bible with the boys and his informal, voluntary Bible Class on Sunday evenings. He has the power to bring the Bible to life and this greatly increases the impression upon the minds of the pupils. The application of the teachings of the New Testament to modern life are illustrated very clearly so that the pupils readily perceive the principles underlying the axiom of "doing to others as you would be done by".

A new prefect, when appointed, took the oath with hand uplifted in the presence of the whole school as he said, "I promise to do my best to uphold the honour of the school." In view of this oath, it is odd that Mr. Ince-Jones never considered the possibility of taking up the popular Scouting venture that was spreading throughout the country in those days.

Apart from doing the administration work of his School and the teaching duties, Mr. Ince-Jones attended many meetings of the NATD and was one of its first campaigners on Higher Education for the Deaf. He gave his maiden speech in 1913 at the NATD Conference at Manchester and he seconded the proposed resolution which read:-

...that in order to complete the system of education for the deaf of this country, it is desirable that some provision for advanced education and higher training in various pursuits should be established and be available to the deaf after school age.

It was put to the vote and was unanimously accepted.

The earliest successful examination results show that Eric Hodges was the first Springhillian to pass the Oxford Junior examinations in 1914 and was followed by Arnold Banks two years later. These results led Mr. Ince-Jones to opt for the new School Certificate examination syllabus in 1917 and his School prospectus was amended to include the new list of public examinations, namely the Junior and the Senior Oxford Local Examinations, and to state that the special aim of the School was to give deaf boys an advanced and varied education as hearing children had in a normal secondary school. At both levels, subjects normally taken at Spring Hill were Composition, English Grammar, Literature (often any Shakespearean play), History, Geography, Religious Knowledge, Arithmetic, Botany with Allied Chemistry and Physics, and Drawing.

Boys who sat the Oxford Local examinations were taken to local schools in June and December. A perusal of a paper on English Essay set for one of the Oxford School Certificate Examinations reproduced in Appendix 3, gives an idea of the range of language which deaf boys had to have in order to gain a pass. In July 1921 both Alexander Bilibin and Frederick Smallman received their Junior Certificates. In 1925 both Oliver Cayley and Eric Hodges were the first boys to be awarded the Senior School Certificates. These results show that some of Ince Jones's pupils proved themselves capable of reaching higher standards. Since boys were not selected from an intellectual point of view, successes of the School were really remarkable. Teachers of the deaf in the United Kingdom began to take notice of Mr. Ince-Jones's successes and admitted

N.A.T.D. CONFERENCE, GLASGOW, 1913.

A group of boys with Mr. Ince-Jones at Spring Hill, 1927
Courtesy of Derek Pritchard

Spring Hill tennis players, 1928
Back Row: Kenneth Pritchard, Donald Denison, Bernard Pitcher, Stanley Powell
Front Row: Lyonel Pritchard, Dick Murphy, Jack Murphy
Courtesy of Derek Pritchard

that there was the evidence of the possibilities of higher education for the deaf. (See Appendix 3 for the list of boys who achieved their examination results.)

Mr. Ince-Jones remembered with pleasure that when he appeared on the school grounds, one boy, who had just sat his examinations, saw him and rushed across from the tennis court where he was playing and said "Oh, we had a lovely paper on *As You Like It*."

Mr. Ince-Jones reminded teachers of the deaf in a certain meeting about the approved resolution on Higher Education for the Deaf in 1913 and reinforced it by saying that:-

As far as possible, I try during the last few years of a boy's school life, to prepare the way for his profession or his business. For example, boys intended for farming or horticulture, study the principles of agriculture, chemistry and botany, as well as general subjects. An embryo architect has special lessons in building construction and architecture.

For example, Fergus Peacocke, totally deaf from birth, was the son of an Archdeacon. He could easily have passed the School Certificate at school, having already passed the Oxford Junior well, but he had exceptional ability in carpentry and decided to take up cabinet-making, for which there is no special advantage in public examinations. His great skill in aeroplane construction was very valuable and in his spare time he learned to fly.

Mr. Ince-Jones commented that

"*surely true education is a preparation not merely for employment but for life as a whole.*"

Lyonel Pritchard gave an idea of Mr. Ince-Jones's speech-teaching and lipreading lessons:-

Mr. Ince-Jones was fluent in speech, with great organising ability. He was easy to lipread no matter at what speed, and was capable of understanding the problems of being deaf. He would not listen to any argument for signing and finger-spelling, though he was willing to teach us finger-spelling for use in any emergency when we had left school. A very personal view of him, however, makes me add that quite honestly we all feared him; he had a very poor teacher-pupil relationship in this respect – and he dominated us that it naturally had its effect when we went out by ourselves to face the open world. Whatever his influence, his favourite subject was to teach speech and lipreading exercises. He enjoyed "experiments," utilizing various noises and teaching English language and its writing.

Examinations of our progress in speech were held at the end of every Easter term. Sometimes friends or business acquaintances of Mr. Ince-Jones came to form a panel and listened to us speaking or as we read from notes or answered questions by lipreading. We always thought that members of the clergy and the Mayor's party were the worst to put up with! Though actual judging was in the hands of the teaching staff, I can always remember a notable visitor at one of these examinations was the Bishop of Leicester. We practised co-ordinating drill and marching with the pronunciation of syllables e.g. Northampton. For NORTH we simply put the left foot forward, for AMP we reached the right foot out and at the same time dropped both hands on to the right thigh, then bringing the feet together and straightening up for TON. Since Mr. Ince-Jones believed in teaching his pupils to speak with a normal voice, we had to work hard on a variety of tones – an angry voice, a calm voice, a raised voice, a lowered voice, etc.

Another impressive way in which we were taught to maintain conversational standards was carried out at meal times, especially at mid-day. Mr. Ince-Jones would always take great care to introduce his pupils to other people so that they could enjoy the opportunity of everyday conversation. For the older boys there was special individual training – we were helped with particular difficulties, small mouth movements were emphasised with distinct phrasing and close syllable control. We were shown the difficulties in the way of lipreading which might come from face-pulling or sudden movements of the head; we were constantly helped to understand the art of approaching all sorts of people that we would come across. His success in this work, of course, came from his understanding of the psychology of deaf people – he well knew the curious nature which seemed to develop in those who had been deaf from an early age – he frequently spoke of this "suspicion" which the deaf person seemed to have of the hearing world. His understanding was so remarkable that it is all the more a pity he never wrote down all he knew.

We often had games of lipreading and speech, and mostly held after Sunday evening school. We had to learn to lipread from profiles, when a screen hid part of the face or chin or even just the side of the mouth. One exercise was when we had to lipread from a shadow thrown in profile on a blank wall. The difficulties we might meet in lipreading a stammer, lipreading at a distance or even the distortions caused by false teeth, were given practice and exercise.

Articulation was the keynote throughout in all school lessons and at meal times; supper time was the only period we were not supervised – we had our own meal, bread and butter provided by the school, tuck from our own resources. Perhaps I remember we did get a bit wild, but this was almost our only relaxation.

Before the advent of mechanical hearing aids the Multitone Company worked at school sometimes and helped Mr. Ince-Jones who tried many experiments. One amplifier was a glorified ear trumpet with room for about eight to listen at one time from various fixed tubes.

Following up Lyonel's comments on the progress on aids for hearing, it was reported in 1929 that:-

Ever since he [Ince-Jones] had had a school he had experimented with a double ear tube exercising both ears. However that was a great strain on the voice and he had recently been using a multiphone by which twelve boys could be exercised at once. He practised for ten weeks on twenty-three boys once or twice a day. One could hear shouting, four could hear a little, while two failed to hear anything. The remainder were practically stone deaf, and yet they all responded. After ten days he gave a test of five vowels and five short sentences and he gave marks. Then he continued to exercise with all sorts of things for seven or eight weeks and after that he repeated the same tests as before only in a varied order. He found that all except one boy had improved, while two of them had improved 100 per cent. He turned down one boy but that boy begged and begged to be allowed to try again and he had improved tremendously...The children were immensely interested, but he could not say how far it would go because as yet it was only an experimental stage. However he personally thought it would improve speech considerably, was full of possibilities and might be revolutionary.

Raymond Thorpe

Arriving at Spring Hill in May 1921 from the station by a horse-drawn cab, the 11-years-old Raymond Thorpe (1921 – 1928) and his mother met Mr. Ince-Jones in his study. Then Raymond was introduced to the Pritchard brothers, Lyonel and Kenneth, who took him to meet other boys. He immediately saw them signing or making gestures which startled him. He wrote in his book *Torpy*:-

It was noticed that the teachers were strictly against signing and fingerspelling but in spite of that the boys carried on with signing when the teachers were out of sight. Often the teachers were cunning and hid behind trees or doors, etc., then they came into our view acting like monkeys chattering which really amused and confused me. They asked those who were signing for their punishment books. It must be pointed out that the boys' signings were not the system recognised by the British Deaf Association.

The matron, Miss Whiting, was short and middle aged with a big bosom, but motherly to boys. She despised Mr. Ince-Jones for being a bully to some of the boys. She retired two years after my arrival at school. She did look after us well when we were in trouble or when not being well. Another matron, Miss Kirby, was appointed but her nature was nothing like the previous matron.

During my first term, I was placed in the junior class under the supervision of Miss Knowles, who was round sixty years of age. She was very strict with a stern looking face and never smiled or laughed. She always appeared to be grinding her teeth. When out for walks, she always carried an umbrella whatever the weather was and led by her mongrel dog called Dandy. It was often tormented by older boys when it was chained to its kennel placed in the yard far away from the house and school buildings.

In those days there were no proper swimming baths like those at the present time. We had to bathe in a pool which was diverted from the River Nene. It was partitioned off with closed boarded fences including cubicles and platforms with diving boards. The water was not purified

All Saints' Church, Northampton.

and not clean. We often see fish swimming around us. Unfortunately I could not swim more than a few strokes as I had cramps in my legs.

The teachers were very strict with our reading lessons during our homework in the evenings. On the following mornings, they asked us questions about what we had read and they expected us to reply in exactly the same words as mentioned in the books. I personally do not agree with that system, as it did not encourage us to express in our own language.

One day, when reading "The Tale of Two Cities" by Charles Dickens, Mr. Ince-Jones asked me to act like Charles Darnay, a character in the story and Jack Attwood, another boy, to play the part of Lucy Manette and to fall in love with each other. Mr. Ince-Jones said to me that I would not get a wife so I retaliated and said to him 'You were too slow to get a wife' which made him feel embarrassed. At lunch time, he mentioned this to his newly wedded wife and she replied to me 'Yes I do agree with you ha ha!!' which made her husband blush badly in front of boys and staff.

There were no provisions for supplying hot water for washing our faces and hands and only lukewarm water for our baths which were taken in turns.

Boys of all creeds and those from homes with no conspicuous religious faith were taught *the great verities together, untroubled by sectarian differences*. The Catholic boys often had special lessons from their priests who knew little about problems of the deaf and, as a result, they learned very little.

Nearly all the boys who were members of the Church of England were confirmed at school by the various Bishops of Peterborough. Much of the preparation was given by Mr. Ince-Jones privately in his study out of school hours.

Getting ready for church
Courtesy of Philip Gibbons

Walking from Spring Hill to the All Saints' Parish Church was a regular routine on Sundays from 1913 to 1945. Out of all the churches in Northampton, the All Saints' Parish Church was chosen for a special reason. Mr. Ince-Jones's uncle, Dr. Arthur H. Jones, was a well-known physician in Northampton and played a major role in setting up the crippled children's home in Northampton. He attached himself to All Saints' Parish Church and became its licensed Lay-Reader. After his death in February 1901, a 27 inches high memorial bronze cross on an octagonal base as a tribute to him was placed in the middle position on the altar.

Raymond Thorpe continued:-

What amused me was that every Sunday during autumn and winter, all boys, even kids of five years old had to wear bowler hats. We, seniors, dreamed of becoming stockbrokers in the future. As a matter of fact we did learn on how to buy and sell shares by Mr. Ince-Jones. During summer, we wore straw hats and starched stiff collars on Sundays and, whatever our religion, we were shepherded to All Saints Church by Mr. Ince-Jones. It was very boring for us as we could not follow the service as we had no interpreters. We had to sit on chairs, in twos in the aisle between the pews while Mr. Ince-Jones sat in the pew facing us. The infants and juniors sat in the balcony with one of the teachers.

Mr. Ince-Jones used to offer a standing prize of 2/6 to any boy who could follow enough of the gist of the sermon to tell him about it. The prize was but rarely won. He admitted it was a severe test for boys.

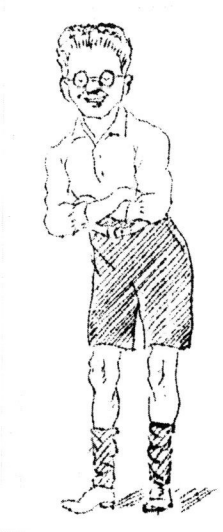

Raymond Thorpe

Raymond Thorpe continued :-

One Sunday after the service, when the choir boys passed us on both sides on their way to the vestry, an Irish boy, Wynne Coates, who sat next to me, accidentally knocked the big silver tray with the morning's collection off the carrier's hands. Money rolled all over the floor; several went into the heating ducts through the perforated iron gratings much to the congregation's amusement. We had to stay to pick up the coins and notes. Mr. Ince-Jones, when back at school, was very annoyed with the poor Irish boy. He often frightened us when he was in an impatient mood and was very temperamental in many ways.

On the last day before leaving school, after having changed clothes for tennis, Lyonel and I were the first to be on the lawn and found a stray bullock grazing. It had escaped from the cattle market about a mile away from the school. So I told Lyonel to open one of the classroom doors and we drove the bullock by twisting its tail into the classroom and closed the door and walked back to the tennis lawn. Later, Mr. Ince-Jones, not knowing anything about the incident, went into the classroom and was confronted by the bullock. It stampeded out of the classroom and disappeared down the road after having knocked several desks and chairs over, dropping dung on the books, etc. A couple of charwomen were called in to clean up the mess. Even to this day Mr. Ince-Jones has not found out that we were the culprits.

Before boys left school, Mr. Ince-Jones and teachers never helped them to prepare facing the hearing world and the selection of careers suitable for them. They never mentioned the word DISCRIMINATION! On the day I left Spring Hill, Mr. Ince-Jones said to me "You would never get a better job than being a road sweeper."

Phillip Gibbons (1927 – 1932) passed his Oxford Junior examinations, but did not get the School Certificate because he did not pass the foreign language paper. He left for the tailoring trade

Philip Gibbons

and, after a while, he decided to take a course in order to become a missioner with the deaf. He studied at King's College, London in 1937, where he took Greek, Ethics, Church History, Old and New Testament and Theology. He found the work difficult, but he eventually became a licensed Lay-reader. He remembered his times at Spring Hill and wrote:-

The oral method of speech and lipreading was strictly carried out. Signing was not allowed. One boy asked Mr. Ince-Jones why he did not allow boys sign. He replied "Your father and mother paid me to teach you to speak and lipread."

Uniform is usually black coats and striped trousers worn as best clothes on Sundays, also for sports white trousers and dark green blazers. Bowler hats were used in winter and straw hats in summer. Some boys complained that boys outside made fun of them because of the hats and they asked for the abolition of the ruling on hats. The reply was that the school aimed to be on the line of public schools like Harrow.

Boys were allowed to use bicycles to go to parks for football or cricket. Every Wednesday senior boys went for a cycle tour to villages outside of Northampton with Mr. Ince-Jones in front. They rode in a crocodile, one boy, talking to another boy behind, knocked down a tramp in front.

In All Saints Parish Church on Sundays, we heard no word of prayers and sermons nor singing of hymns, we had no help to follow the services. The vicar of the church used to drop in school one evening to have a chat with the boys. He played chess with one boy. Mr. Ince-Jones dropped in by chance to see us and he was annoyed to see the vicar. He asked us to tell him when the vicar came in again.

Boys posing on the Spring Hill lawn
Back Row: P. Fischer, L. Pritchard, _____
Front Row: K. Pritchard, J. Copley
Courtesy of Derek Pritchard

Philip Gibbons continued:-

Every year we had a cross-country run, we started at school, down the hill, along the river, up the hill and back to school. Jack Hill from Scotland won every time and some boys were lagging far behind. Mr. Ince-Jones followed in his car with a boy with a heart trouble sitting with him.

Jack Hill.

The school was dominated by Mr. Ince-Jones's personality. He was strict and fair. He showed patience and attention to the boys and usually produced the best out of them. Some boys saw his softer side; they knew they could always go to him when things went wrong. It was noted that

Mr. Ince Jones' breezy and encouraging manner secured good relationship between him and his pupils. All members of the staff showed sympathy, tact and firmness thus creating an exceedingly happy working atmosphere.

Such outstanding results by boys at Spring Hill School put Mr. Ince-Jones in the limelight. He was a colourful personality with a lot of charisma and was fashion-conscious. At some congresses or meetings of teachers of the deaf he wore a silk top hat and with this hat he could be spotted quickly in group photographs. In 1920 he was involved with the Executive Committee of the newly established National College of Teachers of the Deaf (abbreviated NCTD), which was an amalgamation of two old teaching associations of the deaf (CTDD and NATD). He then became the Chairman of the Examining Board of the NCTD and was the Examiner on *History of the Education of the Deaf* questions. His reputation grew and so did that of his Spring Hill School.

Various newspaper headlines on the Spring Hill School's successes in the Oxford Local Examinations in 1928 - 1929

Daily Chronicle (8/9/1928)

DEAF SCHOLARS' ACHIEVEMENT.

SEVEN BOYS PASS OXFORD LOCALS.

An extraordinary example of what can be accomplished by deaf and dumb people is reported from Northampton, where seven pupils of Mr. Ince-Jones' school for deaf boys have passed the recent Oxford local examinations, one the Senior and six the Junior.

These boys, who are nearly all deaf, cannot speak in the ordinary way, but they have acquired speech and understand the speech of others by lip-reading.

The boys took such subjects as French, botany, chemistry, physics, arithmetic, history, geography and several branches of art. All except one boy passed in every subject.

Mr. Ince-Jones' usual comments to any newspaper reporter:-

Discussing this remarkable feat with a Press Association reporter, Mr. Ince-Jones said, "Several of the boys came to me at the ages of five and six. They could not speak a word, could not hear a sound, but worse still, they had no knowledge of any language. The deaf child has no language at all. He has to be taught every word and phrase in connection with objects and actions. It is a very laborious process to build up a knowledge of our own language and only after that has been done can come the subjects of an ordinary school."

Mr. Jones said that although the boys cannot sing or play they can chant the school song, and give three cheers for their opponents after a cricket or football match.

CLEVER DEAF AND DUMB BOYS.

SCHOOL HONOURS DESPITE AFFLICTION.

DEAF BOYS IN THE OXFORD LOCALS

POSSIBILITIES OF SECONDARY EDUCATION.

DUMB SCHOLARS

Remarkable Examination Record of Small School.

REMARKABLE FEATS BY DEAF AND DUMB BOYS.

Afflicted Northampton Lads Pass Stiff Examinations.

THEIR PITIFUL START IN LIFE.

TRIUMPH OVER DEAFNESS.

DEAF & DUMB SCHOLARS' SUCCESS.

TRIUMPH OF MODERN EDUCATION.

Chapter 4

Mr. Ince-Jones in his Prime (1930 – 1938)

Mr. Ince-Jones gave an amusing anecdote:-

My grandfather, who was a Baptist minister, had a parrot which he and his daughter had trained to say with amazing distinctness certain phrases. One of them was "Are you a Baptist?" One day a worthy dean came to call and was ushered into an apparently empty drawing room. In a corner in a cage covered by a cloth, was the parrot. Suddenly out of the silence, in accents clear and imperative came the words. "Are you, are you, are you a Baptist?"
When the very Rev. Gentleman had recovered from his surprise and discovered the origin of the searching question, even he did not suspect the bird of any approximation of ecclesiastical differences. It possessed speech without language.

On the importance of language, Mr. Ince-Jones wrote:-

Some readers may wonder if so much stress is laid on the importance of language, if it is admitted that the teaching of language by speech and that lipreading is probably slower and more tiring to both teachers and pupils, (the latter of whom find pantomime attractive) why the hardest approach to this necessary end is advocated. There are many reasons:-
1. *The deaf person if taught to speak intelligibly and to lipread the speech of others can take his place in the normal society with comparatively slight embarrassments. The signer cannot.*
2. *Very few ordinary people understand the sign language and so their communications are limited to writing and their social life is restricted to the deaf.*
3. *The sign language varies from place to place. It has nothing like the same universality sometimes attributed to it, even among the deaf.*
4. *The language of signs is a distinct language of its own. The order of the words is often quite different from that in spoken and written language. A deaf boy, wishing to sign the sentence "I saw a fat man" would probably start with a sign for the word "man", followed by another for "fat" and ending with "I saw". His sentence then would be "Man fat I saw," Thus for writing and reading it must be a constant process of translation into ordinary language and save confusion.*

Signs are often ambiguous. I cannot recall a case of defamation by slander in signs, though a chalked image on a wall or a wax effigy has been held to be a libel.

Mr. Ince-Jones emphasised that

Speech and language are not synonymous. Possession of wide flexible language is vital because it is the only way by which the mind is liberated. There are various forms of language by which mental life can be awakened in spite of deafness. Whatever the method used, the goal must be language.

Mr. Ince-Jones wrote about the suppression of signing at Spring Hill:-

The habit of signing is almost as natural to the deaf as breathing, but, for all that, it is a menace to an oral school.

The language of signs, vivid though it may be, corrupts spoken and written language. The words are put in the wrong order or left out and so accurate, verbal expression is damned. Yet because of its naturalness, it is very difficult to eliminate. One persistent signer, a new arrival, may corrupt the others and often the worst offender had the least need to sign.

There is no signing at Spring Hill during school hours or while there was supervision but it would be folly to say the boys never on any account signed while they were alone. We did reduce it to a minimum by encouraging everybody to be keen to behave just like other human beings and to regard signing as not the thing. In that they were supported by the prefects, when they were good.

One of Mr. Ince-Jones's many interests was reading books. Regarding the reading scheme adopted in his School, the aim was for any boy to reach the required level of reading before he could be prepared to take public examinations. An extract from Mr. Ince-Jones's paper on Higher Education read:-

He must reach a certain standard... He should have read intelligently, and be able to reproduce such stories as the abridged copies of "Oliver Twist," "Coral Island," "Christmas Carol," "Swiss Family Robinson," "A Tale of Two Cities," and have formed the habit of reading other such books of his own accord ...

Both Mr. Ince-Jones and Mr. Mundin always strove to implant the habit of reading in boys. "Read more books!" was their cry. Their message to the boys was:-

READ, READ, READ! By reading you learn more about life, increase your knowledge and improve your language. Because of deafness you cannot hear what great people say, but by books and papers you can know, as well as anybody, what the greatest people have said. Use your dictionaries. Learn new words and phrases. Read novels because they help you with conversation and give you a good idea of what people do. Read, Read, Read!

Boys were allocated three quarters of an hour's quiet reading on Monday afternoons. Newspaper reading was also encouraged. For example, Alistair Fisher and Christopher Ham read *The Practical Motorist*, John Cobley read *The Evening Standard*, Saville Wallace read *The Daily Express*, Christopher Ham read *The Daily Mirror* and John Wright read *The Morning Post*. On Sunday *The Observer* was read.

Mr. Ince-Jones promised to give any boy sixpence for each book he read on condition that he wrote a brief description of the story.

So far he has paid out about ten shillings! No boy will be allowed to earn more than five shillings in this way! This opportunity is unfortunately not extended to Saville Wallace, Alistair Fisher and John Wright who read so much that Mr. Ince-Jones would soon be bankrupt if they were included!

Mr. Ince-Jones referred to the difficulty of getting suitable reading books for the juniors at the Liverpool NCTD Conference in 1934 and said:-

...One of the greatest difficulties is that there are so few ordinary books in which the language is simple and the subject matter of sufficient interest. Boys of 14 do not want to read about "Dear little Pussy-cat". There is a great opportunity for somebody to re-write famous stories in really simple language.

The juniors were permitted to read comics, but Mr. Ince-Jones had other ideas. He gave them new booklets to read after dinner. When they finished them, Mr. Ince-Jones had more booklets for them! He found a series of four reading books, "*The Basic Reading Books*", admirable and well illustrated. In addition to these elementary readers, a number of classics, put into basic English version, (for example, *Lamb's Tales from Shakespeare*, *Robinson Crusoe*, *Black Beauty* and *St. Mark's Gospel*) were used. After that, further books and newspapers were read with the help of *The Basic English Dictionary* and the *General Basic Dictionary*. Further to encourage the development of language, a series of six Language books, "*From Basic to Wider English*", was used.

Once the boys had obtained the habit of reading and had their elementary language established, they proceeded to learn about the abstract qualities. Mr. Ince-Jones found it useful to lay a foundation starting with good and bad personal qualities, for example, a simple story about bravery and cowardice, and to ask questions such as:-

Was he a kind boy?
What sort of a boy was he?
What bad quality did he show?
What was he punished for?

Regarding the use of idioms, Mr. Ince-Jones wrote:-

In my earliest days I used to work on a long list of about 400 of these idioms, drawn up by my illustrious predecessor, the Rev. Thomas Arnold and classified into four sections according to their supposed difficulty.

For example,   at haste
*   in time*
*   steal a march on*
*   marching of a month*

It was somewhat a dreary process to deal with about eight idioms per lesson and I found it much better to explain the idioms as they cropped up in the course of reading or in conversation, and there were plenty of them every day.

Mr. Ince-Jones knew the importance of idioms in ordinary speech and used them a lot in his conversations with the boys. He pointed out, for example, that "cut" was a basic word and so was "short", but the understanding of them might not mean "cut short his life" anymore than "hold your tongue" or "shut up". In the Language books explaining the meaning of basic words, two examples were given of the use of the word "over":

      (1) with a picture of an umbrella OVER the head;
      (2) with some glass OVER a picture;

but in one of the basic readers there was a phrase such as "his jumping days are OVER." Here was a special use of the word "over," meaning "finished," which had not been explained. Both Mr. Ince-Jones and Mr. Mundin, who always kept the value of language teaching uppermost in their minds, found experimenting with sentences having words of varying meanings to be very desirable and wrote them on the blackboard.

Mr. Mundin arranged with the Librarian of the Northampton Public Library to lend the School forty books at the beginning of every term and a senior boy would be appointed the school librarian.

Mr. Mundin's speciality was the teaching of Geography. The following lessons give an idea of how he carried them out in action. Visits to places in the town were planned and boys were engaged on the idea "*We only see what we know.*" In one particular lesson the words "public" and "private" were introduced and brought out a list of the main public buildings in the town, for example, the Town Hall, Public Library, Central Police Station, Fire Station, General Post Office, Art Gallery and Museum and Technical College. Then the object of the first visit to the town was to see these buildings, making a point of going into each to discover its public nature. On one occasion, Mr. Mundin and his class met the Chief Constable at the Central Police Station, and, to the delight and awe of the boys, he invited them into his private room and showed them revolvers, truncheons, automatic pistols and a catapult confiscated from a local miscreant. He slipped a pair of handcuffs on one of the boys, but the speed with which he wriggled out of them and his triumphant expression astounded the onlookers as he handed them back to the Constable. This incident showed the educational value of such a visit and it was an experience which no classroom teaching could have produced. This visit was followed up with a discussion. Then there was a talk about the route which the class took, for example, "We turned left at the traffic lights" and so on. The streets crossed were found and the buildings visited were marked on a street map of the town with which each boy was provided.

Visiting the public parks was another activity language lesson. Among the new words learned were "tennis courts, bowling greens, putting courses, hire, charge, admission, restaurant, balcony, avenues, shrubs, flower-beds, bandstand." The parks visited were coloured green on the maps and the routes to and from them were traced.

A visit to the Police Court, in which such words as "summoned, bench, magistrates, defendant, witness, dock, guilty, sentenced," were needed to be learned naturally, led to a mock trial in the classroom for reinforcement:-

Mr. Ince-Jones acted as the Judge. Jack Hill was charged with murdering Gordon Paton in the playground. He pleaded "Not guilty". Mr. Mundin, the prosecutor, declared that the prisoner had been seen quarrelling fiercely with Gordon in the playground. Screams had been heard that night. Next morning a large pool of blood was found in the playground and a blood-stained hammer was discovered in Hill's possession. The hammer (smeared with red paint!) was shown to the judge and jury. Saville Wallace and Neville Coughlan gave evidence against the prisoner. At that time things looked very black for the prisoner.
Then, Bernard Pitcher, the defending counsel, stood up and asked that Neville should be sent out of the court while he cross-examined Saville. His lordship granted this request, and the other witness was questioned. He stated that he heard screams at nine o'clock but later Neville said he heard screams at midnight! Both witnesses seemed rather confused. Bernard then made a speech to the jury and pointed out that no body had been found so that no-one knew whether Gordon was dead or not. After retiring, the jury returned a verdict of "Not Guilty" so Jack Hill was discharged. Thus ended an amusing mock-trial.

The boys often watched old silent films because of the captions. Whenever Mr. Ince-Jones took them to the picture-house to watch "a talking film", he tried to give the gist of the story beforehand and, when they had seen it, he gave them a detailed account afterwards.

Shakespearian plays such as *The Merchant of Venice*, *A Midsummer Night's Dream*, *Julius Caesar* and *As You Like It* were read as part of the public examinations in literature. Sometimes boys who studied them were taken by Mr. Ince-Jones in his car to Stratford on Avon to watch the plays. They had front seats in the stalls. As they were familiar with the characters and their order of appearance and they had learned by heart some of the famous speeches, Mr.

Ince-Jones claimed that they "followed almost everything." They were able to do so because they had been prepared beforehand. He stressed that:-

Lipreading is an admirable medium of education, it provides a natural means of communication which makes for normal social life and is sometimes astoundingly successful, but for heavens sake let it never be thought that sight can completely take the place of hearing.

The School premises were maintained now and then. The porch in front of Spring Hill House, the hall and landings were all re-decorated before the new term started. The inner walls of the Schoolroom were painted primrose yellow for the upper part and green for the lower part.

Carpentry Class, 1932
Standing: P. Gibbons. S. Wallace, P. Lewis, B. Pitcher, J. Hill, Mr. Mundin, K. Pritchard
Sitting: J. England, _____, J. Cobley, A. Fisher, C. Ham
Courtesy of Philip Gibbons

Kenneth Pritchard

Mr. Edgar L. Mundin still lived with his father, whose cabinet-making firm continued to thrive at Abington Street. For carpentry lessons, furniture making was the main theme, but sometimes for a change the senior boys made various mahogany boxes for jewellery, an oak cabinet and an oak bookcase. Sometimes they spent the first lesson of the term repairing a number of desks and chairs from the Schoolroom – *a valuable exercise.* Mr. Dixon's old desk, which was made in 1891 at Wickham House, was still used by Mr. Ince-Jones in the Schoolroom in 1936.

Mr. Mundin married Miss Elsie Waterhouse in August 1935 and their new home was at 18 Hillcrest Ave, Northampton.

With the help and encouragement of Mr. Baxter, four attractive posters in bright colours were drawn and painted by four boys and pasted above the blackboard in the big Schoolroom. They were entitled "Science" by Bernard Pitcher, "Potteries" by Dick Murphy, "Transport" by Lyonel Pritchard and "Speed" by Kenneth Pritchard. An Honours board was also designed by Kenneth Pritchard, framed in oak in the workshop, and hung over the fireplace in one corner of the Schoolroom. *These pictures have brightened the room.*

The Arnold Way

School magazines

The first issue of the *Spring Hill Magazine* was launched in December 1930. It was edited by the senior boys, namely, Bernard Pitcher, Dick Murphy and Kenneth Pritchard, who also carried out the printing. The cover was designed by Kenneth Pritchard. There were six issues of the magazine for the first year, but after that, the magazine was published three times a year. The prefects had to collect articles and edit them. The draft was then passed on to Mr. Mundin for proof-reading and finally to Mr. Ince-Jones for his approval. Once approved, Mr. Mundin typed up the draft on stencils and the senior boys printed them and finished off by stapling them. They were then distributed to Old Boys, parents, School patrons, supporters, Staff and boys.

Later the junior boys were encouraged to contribute their articles to the magazine. They found the language of the senior contributors a bit above their heads, but enjoyed Oliver Cayley's and Freddie Davey's cartoons.

Alistair Fisher

When measles and scarlet fever forced the closure of the School three weeks before Easter in 1934, Mr. Mundin was ill and was unable to work on the draft magazine. Alistair Fisher was the only member of the editorial staff who was fit and he took immediate action and produced the *Spring Hill Magazine* single-handedly. He undertook the long task of printing over 70 copies, one page at a time and 20 pages each copy. He printed the magazine cover, cut a stencil for the cartoon, assembled the pages, bound the copies and even addressed the wrappers enclosing the magazines, ready for the post. Mr. Mundin praised Alistair because he thought it was impossible to print the magazine in time. In the following year the magazine with photographs was for the first time printed professionally with by Messrs. J. Stephenson Holt, printers, of Northampton.

Alistair Fisher (1926 – 1935) passed both the Oxford Junior and School Certificate examinations. He returned to Ceylon. Four years later he was appointed the Superintendent of the Kotswana rubber estate. He was a first class linguist in both Singhalese and Tamil, popular with staff and coolies. He died after a week's illness in October 1943.

One of the many contributions by Alistair Fisher was about the breaking up for the holidays:-

The last two days of the term are an age of suspense to boys and teachers alike, but it is probable that the suspense is greater for the younger generation. Breaking-up from the point of view of most boys begins when three rousing cheers are given for the last preparation of the term. There is a noticeable brightness in the eyes of all the boys and flushed faces show that great excitement reigns within.

The last night but one before the breaking-up day is busily spent in packing trunks. Some boys in their excitement are careless in the way they pack so they go to the matron and say that there is no more room in their trunks. However, the far-seeing matron, suspecting untidiness, bids these fellows start all over again.

Next morning most of the boys are wearing their best or second best clothes, their everyday ones have been packed away. Breakfast over, willing boys help to carry trunks from the various bedrooms to the porch, ready for the luggage van which is to come at half-past-twelve. The suspense is somewhat lengthened when after the usual morning prayers, school takes place. Sad to say some pupils are guilty of inattention which rightly incurs the teacher's wrath, but happily no "Fetch your book!" rings out. The quarter of an hour interval is a pleasant break. During this time the headmaster inspects the woodwork in the workshop. A little more time is spent in catching a ball and chattering.

Three Cheers for the School

The interval is over, so the boys troop into the schoolrooms for an hour's work. To the juniors this is an age but to the seniors it soon passes and then, when the clock strikes twelve, school is over at last. At five minutes past twelve the Head, in gown, walks into the big schoolroom, staggering under a load of prizes. The whole school is assembled for prize-giving. The term and examination marks are read out, accompanied by clapping for good marks and improvement shown on the last term's marks. Whoever obtains a prize is warmly applauded by boys and staff alike. When the last prize is given, the Head makes a short speech wishing all his pupils a happy holiday with plenty of sunshine. He ends by proposing three cheers for the holidays and the cheers echo through the room. The senior prefect then steps forward and proposes three cheers for the Headmaster, his wife and their two children. That finished the second prefect calls for three cheers for the staff and not "The Stuff" as one unfortunate person once said! Strange to say, the prefects appear very popular for three cheers are given for them by some enterprising juvenile.

The next most important item of the morning is the withdrawal of money from the school bank, kindly kept by the Headmaster. The crisp crackling of pound notes can be distinctly heard above the din made by the juniors. "The van has come!" cries a small boy and at once willing hands help to lift some twenty-four trunks into the van. The departure of the trunks is warmly appreciated by everyone, including the Head and his wife!

It is an interesting fact that meals on the last day are more appetising than usual. Most probably the thought of going home has made the boys partial to everything. Dinner is a pleasant meal and the air is filled with the clatter of knives and forks all of which seem pleasant to the ear. After lunch the juniors industriously clean out their desks while some of the seniors go to the town to make last minute purchases such as sweets and papers for the morrow's journey. At four-thirty four tidy prefects knock on the drawing-room door and on being admitted take their places round a table laden with large creamy cakes which make their mouths water – it is the prefects' end-of-term tea with the Headmaster and his wife. The general topic of conversation is holiday plans. Tea over, the Head invites the prefects one at a time to have a talk with him in the study.

When the other boys have finished their tea, they rush back to the schoolroom and enjoy themselves to the full, playing games and talking about the times they are going to have. One boy remarks, "Oh, when will tomorrow come!" Another replies, "Never! Tomorrow never comes!" Somewhat crestfallen the unsuspecting fellow asks, "Why?" "Because tomorrow when it comes is today" is the answer. And so on ...

Supper-time is eagerly awaited. The spirit of generosity is indeed present for there is a general sharing of tuck. Supper over, then youngest seniors go to bed. An hour and a half passes and then the last senior leaves the schoolroom and enters the senior dormitory. Half-an-hour later the lights of the dormitory are out but then begins the suspense of waiting for dawn. In summer when the sun rises as early as three-thirty a restless boy wakes and eagerly looks at his watch, only to discover his error. For a time he tries to lie quietly in order to sleep again and thinking that an hour has passed looks at his watch again, but to his intense disgust, finds it is only five minutes later! Eventually he dozes off and wakes with a start to find that the others are half-dressed.

The atmosphere is most exciting, yet at breakfast everything is quiet except for an occasional clatter of knife and fork. The head tries to engage in conversation but sad to say his advances are not readily accepted. When breakfast is over, the first boys to go away get ready for the journey. Handshakes are hearty all round. The journey by taxi to the station is one big thrill. The familiar smell of the station is extremely pleasant; the puff-puff of goods trains is music to the ear. Once the train steams out of the station, the homeward-bound boys sink limply to their seats, happy and yet strangely sad especially those who are returning to school no more.

The arrival of the fifteen year old Bernard Pitcher (1926 – 1932) at Spring Hill School must surely mark a milestone in British Deaf history for it was he who paved the way for others on their path to higher education. It can be said that what Abraham Farrar did for the Rev. Thomas Arnold, Bernard Pitcher did for Mr. Frederick Ince-Jones.

Bernard Pitcher

At first Mr. Ince-Jones found him immature for his years both mentally and physically, but with a very good retentive memory. After two years at Spring Hill, Bernard successfully gained his Oxford Junior Examinations in 1928. Mr. Ince Jones did not think he was remarkable as there were other boys of the same age in his class far ahead of him. But after such success, he made rapid progress and by the end of 1929 he sat for the Oxford Senior Examinations and passed four subjects, but was one short of the required five passes to obtain the Certificate. The following year he gained six more credits. His subjects were Botany, Arithmetic, Mensuration, French, History of the British Empire, Geography, English, Religious Knowledge, Painting and Model, Flat and Memory Drawing.

Aiming for a University degree in Science, he had to study Higher Chemistry, Physics, Mathematics and Mechanics. For Chemistry and Physics practical work, Bernard attended the local Technical College and gained useful experience. He also received private tuition in mechanics and trigonometry from Mr. Bailey, the head of the said college. In 1932 Bernard passed all the required subjects necessary for admission to the University. In the autumn of 1932 Bernard Pitcher was admitted to the Royal College of Science, part of the University of London, after little persuasion made by Mr. Ince-Jones, who reminded university authorities that Noel Brunning-Maddison, an ex-pupil of Mr. H. N. Dixon, had studied there in 1907 and successfully gained his A.R.C.S. Diploma.

Alexander Bilibin once recited on Bernard Pitcher:- '*Work, work, work*' and signed this by rhythmically chopping the edge of his right hand into the palm of the other. Philip Gibbons showed in action how Bernard hunched over a desk with a book before him with his hands shading his eyes to dispel any distraction, '*Read, read, read.*' Only once had Bernard failed an examination. The day before he sat for it he read in the newspaper that fish was good for the brain, bought two tins of sardines, conscientiously ate every last one of them and was sick all night! Mr. Ince-Jones paid tribute to Bernard and said:-

I may have had pupils more brilliant in some respects, quicker in the uptake and more striking in verbal expression, but never one so patient, courageous, persevering or of more exemplary character. Despite his great success he remains the same quiet, unassuming, conscientious fellow he has always been. His application to work has been magnificent and his retention of knowledge superb.

Mr. Ince Jones had an exceptional decade: the 1930s. He gave talks and campaigned on Higher Education for the Deaf in conferences and branch meetings of the NCTD. He was elected as the Chairman of the NCTD from 1933 to 1934. He produced a masterly analytical summary on the Eichholz Report, "*A Study of the Deaf in England and Wales*", published in 1933. Dr. Eichholz, a highly experienced Chief Inspector of schools for the Deaf, wrote in his Report:-

The capacity of the deaf is very limited. It runs short when abstract ideas of the simplest nature have to be put into words.

It did not really apply to the talented deaf boys at Spring Hill. Mr. Ince-Jones said it was a misleading statement. He pointed out that

The CAPACITY of the deaf, including expression of abstract ideas, is unlimited. What are limited are time and adequate education. The longer school period now provided will grant opportunities which certainly should be utilised.

On October 14 1934 one of Mr. Ince-Jones's most interesting experiences of his life was the time he spent with Miss Helen Keller at her hotel in London and escorted her to a luncheon in her honour at the Holborn Restaurant. He wrote:-

Here was a deaf and blind lady... It was embarrassing to imagine what she would think of me whom she could neither see nor hear. I would hasten to tell her how much we appreciated her kindness and that of Miss Thomson [Helen's secretary and interpreter] *in coming so far to give us pleasure. I hoped it might not be awkward. Never were fears less justified, nor more speedily removed. A radiant person put me instantly at ease. With outstretched hand she cried in perfectly clear speech: "How do you do, Mr. Ince-Jones, I am so pleased to see you."*

We talked together on a very great many subjects. For most of the conversation Miss Thomson interpreted my remarks to her by the one-handed alphabet and Miss Keller

Miss Helen Keller

Meeting of Executive Committee of the National College of Teachers of the Deaf, Margate
SEPTEMBER 29TH, 1934.

Top Row.—Mr. F. L. Denmark, M.A. Liverpool. Mr H. S. Follwell, Stoke (*Hon. Sec.*), Mr. A. Andrews, Leeds. Mr. E. Evans, Gorleston. Mrs. H. Haycock. Mr. E. W. Stannard, London. Miss A. Simmons, Penn. Miss A. Lack, Birmingham. Mr. C. W. Stephens, Doncaster. Mr. F. G. Carter, Brighton. Mr. L. L. Bayliss, Gorleston, Mr. C. G. Goodwin, Stoke (*Hon. Minuting Sec.*).

Middle Row. Miss M. G. Wilkins, Sheffield. Mr. J. H. Blount, Penn. Miss E. Goodwin, London. Mrs. J. H. Blount. Brig. B. L. Beddy, D.S.O. (*School Secretary*). Mrs. H M. Thomson-Barr, Matron. Mr. W. Carey Roe, R.A., Derby. Miss E. Hare, London. Miss D. Kutner, London. Miss D. E. Baker, Birmingham. Mr. H. Haycock (*Hon. Treas.*). Miss A. Metcalf, Leicester. Mr. J. Spalding, Manchester. Miss D. Spencer, Bolton.

Bottom Row. Miss Crogham. Mr. A. B. Swayne, Headmaster (*Vice-Chairman*). Mrs. A. B. Swayne. Mrs. W. Carey Roe. Mr. E. Portlock (*Member of School Committee*). Mr. F. Ince-Jones, B.Sc. Northampton (*Ex-Chairman*). Mr. D. Craig, Doncaster (*Chairman*). Mr. C. Shaw, London (*L.C.C. Inspector of Special Schools*). Miss M. Hare, Burgess Hill. Mr. H. Clegg, London (*Registrar*). Miss H. Davids, London.

replied at once in speech, but at times she read my lips with her fingers. She placed her thumb, first and second fingers on my throat, lips and nose and read remarkably well.

She asked after my own school, clapped her hands when I told her of the success of my old pupil, Bernard Pitcher, at the Imperial College of Science; sent him her best wishes and hoped he would be successful in gaining a degree.

He asked her to say what she found to be her most difficult task. She was able to lipread him without difficulty and replied, "Learning to speak." A further question revealed that her favourite occupation was to read an interesting book. It was truly an unforgettable moment for Mr. Ince-Jones, who paid his tribute to Miss Helen Keller:-

Great in her achievements, great in her spirit. And very great too is that wonderful teacher, Miss Sullivan Macy, who drew this radiant being out of the shadow.

The Vice-Presidency of the NCTD was conferred on Miss Helen Keller.

Abraham Farrar was also elected as the Vice-Presidency of the NCTD for his research on the history of education of the Deaf and for his gifts of rare books, concerned with the deaf, to the Ryland Library, Manchester University. He was and still is the only deaf person to achieve such a distinction.

Bernard Pitcher was duly awarded the degree of the Bachelor of Science with 2nd Class Honours in addition to the A.R.C.S. Diploma. There were headlines on Pitcher's achievement in the local and national newspapers and Mr. Ince-Jones was jubilant.

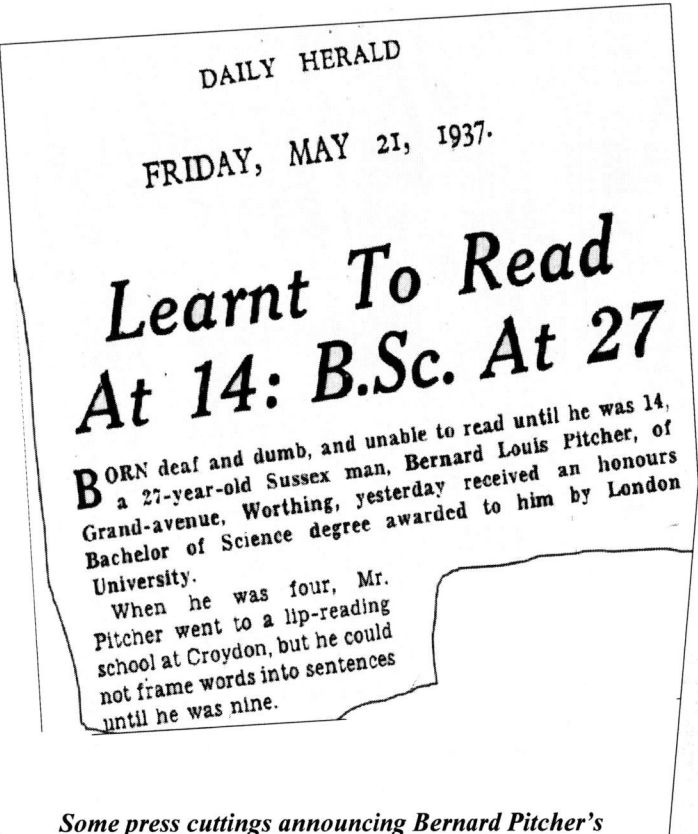

Some press cuttings announcing Bernard Pitcher's academical success in 1937

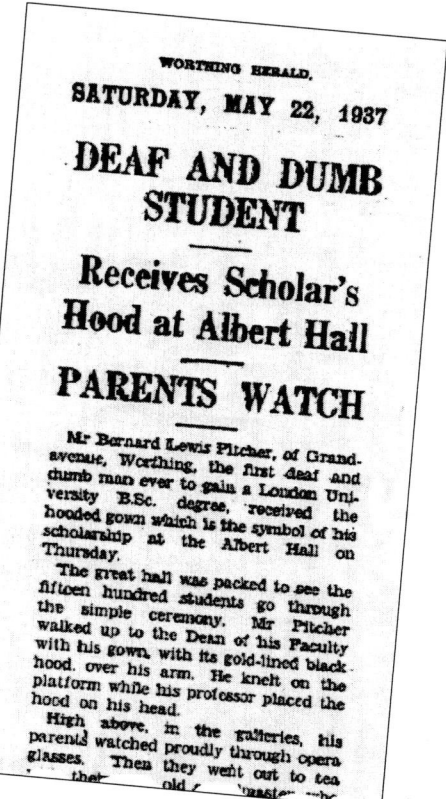

However he was dismayed at the wording referring to Bernard being *DEAF AND DUMB* in many of the newspapers and wrote a letter to the Editor of *The Teacher of the Deaf*:-

> *Spring Hill,*
> *Cliftonville,*
> *Northampton*
> *25/5/1937*
>
> *Dear Sir,*
> *The conferring of a B.Sc. degree upon Mr. B.L. Pitcher at the Albert Hall this week has inspired certain newspapers to well-intentioned but in many respects very inaccurate comments. These included an imaginary interview with myself. I shall be glad if you will allow me in your columns to correct two of these mistakes, which I feel to be important.*
> *Mr. Pitcher is generally described as being unable to speak. This of course is not so. When faced suddenly with an unknown newspaper reporter, he not unnaturally prefers to write down his remarks. Though possibly his speech is not quite so good as when he left school, it is perfectly intelligible and continuously used. He made two excellent speeches at our last Old Boys' Dinner and at the Old Boys' Cricket match. These were understood by everybody. His education throughout has been by speech and lip-reading.*
> *Secondly, I am credited with saying in an interview that he worked fourteen hours a day, presumably at school! Whatever he may have done for a short time at the University on the eve of an examination, he certainly had no chance of working even half these hours at school. Good results are not obtained there by cramming or overworking boys. He played all the usual games, cricket, football, tennis, billiards, etc., had all the usual half holidays and went to bed at 9.30 p.m. His hours of work at school were probably much shorter than those of a boy at an ordinary secondary school.*
> *He is a magnificent worker, enjoys work and good health, but it would be a pity for his superb achievement to be associated with mistaken ideas as to the means of its accomplishment.*
> *Yours truly,*
> *F. INCE-JONES.*

After completing his dissertation entitled "The Upper Valentian Gastropod Fauna of Shropshire" in 1940, Bernard Pitcher was awarded a Ph. D., thus making him the first deaf-born Briton to achieve it. For Mr. Ince-Jones it was a triumph.

The examination results of the boys who successfully passed them were listed in the Spring Hill Magazines as well as on the Board of Roll of Honour (see Appendix 3). This spurred someone to say

John Wright

"These results will give an impetus to the movement to establish a school for the higher education of those pupils from the elementary schools for the deaf who showed the necessary promise but were unable to afford the cost of attendance at a private school."

John Wright (1934 – 1939) was another Springhillian celebrity. Briefly, John was born in Johannesburg in 1920, and at the age of 7 he became totally deaf through scarlet fever. He left South Africa for England to receive private oral tuition by Miss Blanche Neville, an experienced teacher of the deaf. Then on February 23 1934, on his birthday, he and his mother were taken by taxi from the Northampton station to school and found Mr. and Mrs. Ince-Jones welcoming them. John Wright was then led to the Dining Room for supper and what he saw was a picture of another world. Seated round the table were six boys who were freely communicating with each other since no supervisors were present. In his autobiography he described the boys' conversation with him during supper:-

'John Wright. From South Africa. Brown! brown! look, brown! hot! look! BRRROWN! (they were admiring my African suntan...) Sun! Whew! Do you like girls? Shut up! I'm tired of you! I'm talking! ... Shut up! Listen to me! I'm talking to John Wright. Do you like England? Rain, rain, wet, cold, dark, sad, sad...'

Wright's experience led him to say

... the mouthing of words to magnify lip movements for those whose eyes are their ears.

After John's entry had been accepted, Mr. Ince-Jones received a letter from John's South African doctor, who suggested that as a pupil, John would never do much good. Mr. Ince-Jones thought it ridiculous as it did not take long to find that John had a brilliant mind, though his position in ordinary school subjects, except for English, was not high and his interest in sport, art and many other things was negligible, but he only needed to be brought out. His speech required considerable attention and his lip-reading was poor. He had acquired the habit of withdrawing himself and becoming absorbed in his beloved books.

Wright, in the first edition of his autobiography (1969), gave fictitious names to boys who were at supper on his first evening, but twenty years later, in his revised book, the fictitious name *Henry Garnet* gave way to John Napier (1933 – 1938) who was at Spring Hill at the same time as Wright. John Napier received his early education at Oxley School for the Deaf (Miss Taylor's private school at Hatch End, Middlesex) and at Miss Mary Hare's Dene Hollow School, Burgess Hill. Mr. Philip Gibbons, himself an ex-pupil of Miss Taylor's school, remembered him as the boy who had a scratching habit and wore gloves. He also mentioned that Mr. Ince-Jones met John Napier and his parents at the office of the RNID, 105 Gower Street, London, for a possible transfer to Northampton. Thus the fifteen year old John Napier entered Spring Hill School in 1933. Wright wrote about John Napier's use of his signs:-

Rubbing the breast-bone with the tips of the fingers meant 'I didn't do it'...it derived from a gesture used by John Napier, who could utter perhaps three or four words ... The gesture was one of his habits. He would rub his chest in that way while trying to utter the word 'Good'. This meant, or stood for, 'I am a good boy' – which was also his way of saying 'I didn't do it'.

Sign-names were and are almost always used in any school for the deaf and it is not surprising that Wright mentioned them:-

We also had nicknames, non-verbal nicknames ... Because the headmaster wore an eyeglass his 'nickname' became a calliper movement of thumb and forefinger (originally it had been a proper round O made with finger and thumb and applied to the eye) - a shorthand reference to the famous monocle. Or a habit would do – the assistant master, Mr. Mundin, had a trick of fingering his chin... A fist clenched at the back of the head, fingers exploding upwards, became my 'nickname'; this was supposed to imitate the way my unbrushed hair stuck out.

Then Wright recalled some incidents of a daily school routine in the Schoolroom:-

The school stood to attention until Mr. Ince-Jones stalked in, black-gowned, magistral. He would recite the Lord's Prayer which we repeated after him line by line. There were some occasions when he briefly addressed the boys on moral points. At least once a term Mr. Ince-

Jones blew up over the wearing or rather non-wearing of the plain green school tie.

A screen was set up to divide the senior class, taken by Mr. Ince-Jones, from Mr. Mundin's junior class at the warmer end of the room. The infants and the very backwards were looked after by Miss Whitaker in a small separate classroom at the other side of the building.

The ordinary method of demanding attention from a pupil (if he happened not to be looking) was a hard thump of the magistral heel. This could be heard reverberating through the floorboards. Behind the screen Mr. Mundin did the same but his heel thud was toned down. The ink wells on the desks shook a bit.

For mental arithmetic, some of us stood in a semi-circle. Simple sums and problems were fired at them. Mr. Mundin took boys for carpentry. He lived with his father who was a well-known cabinet-maker in Northampton. From his father he inherited a reverential attitude to tools and craftsmanship.

Yes, we had good times; but cabined, cribbed, confined, bound in – for only once a week were we allowed out of the school gates. This was on Saturday mornings, when for a couple of hours we had the freedom of the town to do our shopping. (We got sixpence a week pocket-money.) For the rest of the week we were prisoners.

Patricia and Pamela Ince-Jones had their own pet tortoise George-Elizabeth as well as their cat Ginger. John Wright wrote an ode on the unhappy demise of their tortoise:-

> Seek not for George, for cruel Death
> Hath seized our loved Elizabeth!
> Enhaloed, with industrious jaw
> He masticateth evermore
> The never-ending lettuce leaf!
> For aye consoled from mortal grief!
> O weep no more, for all is well;
> Shielded by the Almighty shell
> Elizabeth can nothing miss
> Encabbaged in Eternal bliss!
> O mind you how we trampled flowers
> In search of George through sunlit hours?
> Removed beyond all earthly pain
> We seek for him (as then) in vain!

In 1936 John Wright passed the Oxford Junior Examination with four Distinctions, more than any hearing school candidate, and was the only candidate who obtained a distinction in Religious Knowledge. He then went to South Africa for a break and returned with a poem reminiscing his days in his native land:-

Retrospect

> I'll think of dusty roads with high winds blowing,
> I'll think of kopjes glinting in the sun,
> I'll think of dusty farms with blue gums growing,
> And oxen coming homeward, one by one;
> I'll think of blue-wombed clouds heavy with thunder,
> And that uneasy wind which stirs parched trees
> Before the lightning splits the skies asunder;

I'll think of jacarandas in the breeze;
I'll think of breaking seas and golden beaches,
I'll think of curling seas and cruddled spume,
I'll think of orchards filled with ripened peaches,
And moonlit sands and their soft milky gloom;
I'll think of swallows and their glancing wings,
And oh, my heart, a thousand tiny things.

Mr. Ince-Jones (on the extreme left) teaching botany to a class of Senior boys in the sunken garden, with John Wright next to Mr. Ince-Jones, 1937

The following year saw John passing brilliantly in the School Certificate examination, obtaining seven credits out of a possible maximum of eight. He had 6 A's, 2 B's and 1 C. One of the A's was for General Literature which required a wide and systematic course of reading. He stayed a further year to take Latin and French with the help of two Grammar School teachers for private tuition. In 1939 he passed the Oxford Senior Local exams and was admitted to Oriel College, Oxford, for a degree course in English. In 1942 he gained his B.A. degree. Another feather in Mr. Ince-Jones's silk top hat! John Wright changed his name to David Wright when he went to Oriel. He became an accomplished poet and wrote several books of poems and was awarded the Honorary Fellowship of Oriel College for his literary work.

In the revised prospectus of Spring Hill School Mr. Ince-Jones wrote on the importance of training pupils to make use of their residual hearing loss. The following examples extracted from the *Spring Hill Magazine* show how this was tackled during the 1930s.

There was a radio in Mr. Ince-Jones's drawing room and it happened that the annual Oxford v Cambridge boat race was being staged in March 1931. The boys were allowed to leave their Carpentry lesson to sit round Mr. Ince-Jones who was listening to the radio and at the same time informing them on the progress of the boat race. One of the lipreaders wrote:-

we could see in our minds the race as it was actually taking place.

In 1934 a new electrical apparatus for hearing, as a substitute for the old multiphone, was purchased.

All of the boys can hear more of it. The instrument consists of an amplifier which looks like an ordinary wireless set, a separate control panel and eight earphones attached to the control panel Each pair of headphones has a small box-like attachment for controlling the volume of sound. On the control panel are eight knobs one for each pair of headphones and by turning these, high tones or low tones can be emphasised. The amplifier can be used for ordinary speech or as a wireless loudspeaker and set. When the set is used for wireless the music can be heard through the headphones. We are using the instrument regularly and are finding it most useful for improving speech. One Friday afternoon when we could not play football, Mr. Mundin let us listen-in to music.

A year later Mr. Ince-Jones bought some Linguaphone gramophone records for the boys. Extracts from the *Spring Hill Magazine* read:-

They listen to them through the multitone. The gramophone is placed near the microphone in the multitone set. They are very interesting and help us a lot with our speech. Seniors often listen to records in the evenings. The records are about the Brown family. Each side has two parts, the first a description of a picture in the Linguaphone book and the second, conversation on the picture.

Every Saturday night Miss Whittaker and the boys who can hear enough, listen-in with the multitone to the First News for the results of football matches. We are keen on football. Each boy has his favourite home team. Gordon [Paton]*'s favourite is the Arsenal, Christopher* [Ham]*'s is Derby County, Bill* [Jenkins]*'s is Cardiff City and Neville* [Coughlan]*'s Stoke City.*

Jack Murphy [an Old Boy] *has set the School Song to music and very good it is. Although he is quite deaf now, he can still compose good music.*

The School Song

The School, the School, the best school we know!
God bless the School, wherever we may go.
We will remember all the friends we've made,
We will be loyal, truthful, unafraid.
The School! The School!
Long live the School!
Hurrah!

George Street is enjoying his work at the Multitone factory. We are sorry to hear of the death of his grandfather, the son of the architect who designed the Law Courts in the Strand, London.

Mr. Ince-Jones remarked on John Wright's handwriting and said that if only John would typewrite his letter, he would be able to read it. So he arranged for some senior boys, including John, to attend a typing school in town every Saturday morning, taught by Miss Harding. Six teenage girls were also present in the class. One day, when boys took swimming at the public swimming pool in Midsummer Meadow, one of the girls from the typing class happened to be there, recognised one of the boy typists and gave a friendly wave to him. One member of the staff saw this incident and reported to Mr. Ince-Jones. Wright recalled:-

The unfortunate lad who had waved back to the girl barely escaped a caning. Outraged to learn that for two months we had actually shared a room for an hour a week with half a dozen nubile girls, albeit chaperoned by the proprietress, the headmaster saw to it that from henceforth we had our typing lessons in a room by ourselves, in purdah as it were.

Punishments given by Mr. Ince-Jones to culprits were carried out by caning. Philip Gibbons remarked that Mr. Ince-Jones sometimes turned a blind eye to any boy's small fault. For instance, Mr. Ince-Jones once saw a boy signing in the playground from his bedroom window on the first floor of Spring Hill House but did not take any action at all. Philip, who was the head prefect in his last year in 1932, said that prefects often punished the boys by smacking their hands with a ruler. Mr. Ince-Jones recalled:-

... only one boy who absented himself. He announced to me that, because he had had some difference between us over some matter of punishment, he should not come to my class and he did not like me. I told him I was sorry but he must please himself. Sure enough, he sat well away from the class and was apparently absorbed in a book. However soon he began to turn glances to my lips and the black board. Gradually he edged nearer. Then he was on the outskirts of the class and though he asked no questions on that occasion, he was very active next Sunday!

On another occasion a senior boy, aged 18 years, from Belfast arrived a day late for the beginning of the term and turned up in the middle of Mr. Ince-Jones's scripture class. Without a word Mr. Ince-Jones rose up from his desk and stalked out of the classroom, signalling the young man to follow him to his study. After questioning him for his lateness, the responses prompted Mr. Ince-Jones to accuse the young man of sleeping out with a woman in London and the punishment was a severe flogging across the young man's bare back. Wright saw the weals on his friend's back the next morning. He indicated that Mr. Ince-Jones would go out of his own way to stamp out any sexual scandal surrounding his School. At night time he would go round the dormitories and suddenly switch the lights on to catch out any boy doing immoral behaviour and caning would follow suit. It is thought that his attitude on the immorality of sex was due to his strict Victorian upbringing, which led him to insist that boys be confined to the School grounds, thus minimising any public damage to the reputation of his School.

When school began towards the end of September 1938, it was thought that war would break out soon. The School was determined to be prepared, however, and Mr. Mundin and some of the boys helped to make the cellar of Spring Hill House gas-proof by preparing a heavy felt curtain to hang across the door. Mr. Ince Jones made sure that the cellar was equipped for any emergency. One day when Mr. Chamberlain, the Prime Minister, announced to the House of Commons that he would fly to Munich, the boys tried on their gas-masks. Each gas-mask was packed by the prefects and the boy's name written on the outside of the box.

Regarding the boarding out for senior boys when the Spring Hill House dormitories were full, Mrs. Strickland normally had boys sleeping at her house. In 1934 she had five boys! Five years later, during the eight weeks' summer vacation, the loft above the big Schoolroom was converted into five new rooms with an additional upstairs lobby, that is, a bedroom for two senior prefects, a bathroom, and a toilet with an Ascot heater, a new classroom and a private study for the prefects. There was also a spare room overlooking the playground. Mr Ince-Jones was ready for the next school year.

Two elite oral London deaf clubs were formed, the National Deaf Club in 1906 and the Spurs Club in 1934, and they served the need for deaf people to get-together for social reasons. Interestingly, some members of these two clubs were from Northampton School for the Deaf. Not only that, forming Old Boys' Reunions and an Old Boys' Cricket Team allowed many Old Boys of Northampton High School for the Deaf to meet each other and to talk of their old days. It was in 1930 that the Old Boys' Reunion was held for the first time in London. The following year saw a repeat held at the Grosvenor Hotel, London, which was a better show than the previous one. After dinner, formal speeches by several Old Boys and free conversations were wholly oral, both signs and fingerspelling being strictly tabooed. Mr. Ince-Jones and Mr. Mundin were present on each occasion and so was Abraham Farrar. Oddly enough, on two occasions, it was recorded that Farrar's prepared speech was read out either by Mr. Mundin or by Alexander Bilibin on Farrar's behalf. Mr. Ince-Jones explained that Farrar could never be persuaded to break his life-long rule not to make a public speech!

In one of Farrar's prepared speeches, he said he was proud to have been associated with the founding of the School but wished he had been born many years later so that he would have enjoyed the amenities at Spring Hill! The Old Boys' Dinner Reunion was then held biennially up to the time of the Second World War when it ceased.

The third Old Pupils' Reunion Dinner at the Grosvenor Hotel, London, November 16 1934

Reading from Mr. Ince-Jones in the centre and round the table to the left:- Mr. Ince-Jones, Abraham Farrar, M. Marshall, John Cobley, Eric J. Hodges, Saville Wallace, Noel G. Brunning-Maddison, Mr. E. L. Mundin, Bernard Pitcher, Sydney Druiffe, Arnold Banks, Alexander Bilitbin, Vivian J. Yorke, Jack Attwood, Charlie Condy

Chapter 5

Out-door Activities

Mr. Mundin the games master brought in the house system in 1929 and in the following year saw the names of the houses, suggested by Oliver Cayley, as Sky Hawks, Rovers, Pirates and Crusaders. Inter-house competitive matches for Cricket, Cross-Country Running, Swimming, Tennis and Football were arranged. As each house contained at most six boys, house matches were played with a permutation of two houses fielding their teams against the other two houses.

The winners of various House competitions proudly wore gold stars in their lapels. Marks were not given just for games however – speech prowess, gardening proficiency, good manners at meal times, good deeds and general conduct – anything which showed improvement could be rewarded.

Cricket

When Mr. Ince-Jones took over the school at 23 East Park Parade in 1909, there were no cricket matches in his first summer term. He had only 8 boys, ranging from 10 to 16 years of age. They practised in the nets and in the open. A challenge to a cricket match was issued to Eaglehurst College, East Park Parade, which had 80 boys on its roll. The school team composed of 8 boys, Mr. Ince-Jones himself, an external student of theology and the 12th man of the opponents. The first cricket match in the history of the School took place. The toss was won and the School batted first. It was dismissed without scoring a run! The School managed to get its opponents out for about 40 runs. In the second innings, the school made 80.

Moving to Spring Hill in 1912, the school increased its roll and it was able to field its own team.

The accounts of School cricket matches against local school teams took up about seven pages of the School magazines and the heading under Cricket notes bore Mr. Ince-Jones as the President! Truly cricket was Mr. Ince-Jones's first love in sports and he played in almost every School match up to the Second World War. He was an all-rounder, and his accurate and economical bowling with good length produced a handful of wickets with few runs now and then.

Annual matches against Mr. J. N Beasley's team, the Northampton Grammar School 2nd XI and Eaglehurst College were a regular feature of the cricket season. For home matches, St. Andrew's Hospital Ground in Billing Road was the usual site with permission to use it from the medical superintendent, but practice took place on the Racecourse.

Mr. J. N. Beasley was an ex-Northants cricket captain and his brother, R. N. Beasley also played for the same county. Mr. Tyler, an ex-county captain, was the usual umpire in School matches against Beasley's team. He died in 1930. They were good friends of Mr. Ince-Jones. Friendly matches between Mr. Ince-Jones's XI and Mr. Mundin's XI were played at Castle Ashby during the "annual holiday". The pitch on the beautiful ground was at the front of the famous mansion.

The Arnold Way

The Old Boys' annual cricket match against the School was also a regular feature and the first match started in June 1930 at St. Andrew's Ground with an easy victory for the School. At the second annual match in July 1931, Mr. Ince-Jones did not play as he had been unwell during the week. "We were sorry that he had to watch his team playing, instead of leading them as he had done for 20 years. This meant that he had captained the School team since 1911! Mr. Philip Gibbons recalled that, during a cricket match, Mr. Ince-Jones skied a ball for a six and the ball struck a lady passing by. He sped towards her and offered her his apologies!

Tea was provided in the pavilion in 1932. Yet another win for the School.

The third Old Boys' annual cricket match in 1932 yielded the result:-

OLD BOYS			SCHOOL		
A. Banks	lbw Wallace	1	E.L. Mundin	c. Murphy b. Banks	60
D. Dension	b. Wallace	6	B. Pitcher	retired	58
L. Pritchard	b. K. Pritchard	33	K. Pritchard	c. and b. Murphy	21
J. England	run out	1	S. Wallace	c. Denison b. Banks	5
O. Cayley	c. Ham b. F. Ince-Jones	8	F. Ince-Jones	not out	27
J. Gibbons	b. Fisher	22	C. Ham	run out	11
D. Murphy	b. F. Ince-Jones	5	B. Voss	b. Bottomley	4
H. Bottomley	c. F. Ince-Jones b. Pritchard	2		Extras	21
A. Bilibin	not out	0		Total for 5 wkts	247
B. Taylor	b. F. Ince-Jones	0	(P. Gibbons, N. Coughlan and P. Lewis did not bat)		
N. Glenn	b. Coughlan	0			
	Extras	10			
	Total	88	The third win for the School!		

Mr. Ince-Jones, a life member of the Northampton County Cricket Club, wrote:-

We have subscribed £1 to the Northampton County Cricket Club Fund. The Club has appealed for subscriptions and we should not like first class cricket to end in Northampton. We have seen many exciting matches and many famous cricketers at the County Ground and hope to see many more.

Mr. Mundin often took some boys to watch County cricket and an account was written by one of them:-

Northampton won the first match against Glamorgan. We read that Adams, a new player for the County, took 4 wickets for 12 runs, thus helping to gain the victory. Mr. Mundin aroused our interest by saying that Adams was at the Grammar School, at the same time as he.

Feverishly we looked through old, tattered scorebooks and at last found that Adams played against Spring Hill on four occasions. His best bowling performance was 4 for 34 but he did not bowl on two occasions. His highest score was 13 which he made twice before being bowled by Mr. Mundin and Pat Fischer respectively. In the last match he was caught for a duck by Mr. Mundin off Pat Fischer's bowling. We wonder what he thought about his friend, Mr. Mundin then!

Mr. Mundin's colleague was Sydney Adams, a leg spinner, who had the unique distinction of taking wickets with his first two balls in first class cricket in a match against Dublin University. Patsy Hendren helped to coach Patrick Fischer and the two Pritchard brothers at the Lord's Cricket Ground during the holidays and thought Patrick's left-handed bowling was good enough for Northamptonshire.

Playing cricket on the lawns of Castle Ashby circa early 1930s
Courtesy of P. Gibbons

In 1927 Patrick Fischer passed his School Certificate examinations with flying colours and left school for South Africa. He passed the final examinations for architecture at Cape Town University and had Dip. Arch. after his name. A year later he was awarded the A.R.I.B.A. diploma and was a qualified architect. Patrick Shillington (previously Fischer) played cricket for his university throughout his time there and won the cup awarded to the best cricketer of the year in 1932. This is remarkable because the cup was won in the previous year by Mr. M. G. Owen Smith, the famous cricket and rugby international and in the following year by Mr. A. Dudley Nourse, jr. afterwards the cricket captain of South Africa. The registrar of the said university wrote to Mr. Ince-Jones that during the year 1932

Patrick Fischer
Courtesy of
D. Pritchard

Pat was the best all-rounder in the Varsity Cricket XI. He would probably have been Captain but for his deafness.

In June 1932, Mr. Mundin, who was a stylish opening bat, scored a century for the first time for the School and produced three more centuries during his stay at Spring Hill. However Mr. Ince-Jones made his first and only century in 1917.

Lyonel Pritchard was an outstanding all-rounder and when he left Spring Hill, he played for Gloucester City Cricket Club as a fast bowler. Kenneth Pritchard was also an all-rounder and when he left, he played regularly for Coolham Village Cricket Club. Lyonel wrote:-

The main summer school game was Cricket and boys were coached by local county players. Games fields were on lease from Northampton Corporation and matches were frequently played with hearing schools or club teams. Since most of the pupils had well-to-do parents they often continued games-coaching in the holidays and I can well remember being coached by Patsy Hendren at his indoor cricket club in London.

In one season Bernard Pitcher scored an undefeated 46 runs in a school cricket match against Northampton Grammar School 2nd XI and 69 not out in another match against Mr. Beasley's XI. In 1932 his batting average was over 70. John Wright was the cricket scorer and remembered Pitcher's performances on the cricket pitch when he saw him batting for the Old Boys against the School and wrote:-

Pitcher was one of the mainstays of the school cricket team. In spite of poor vision (he wore pebble lens) he was a remarkably successful bat. His batting was of a piece with his character – dogged, meticulous, and unbelievably persevering. For every kind of ball, long hop, full toss, short length, good length, leg break, off break, he had one and the same stroke: a perfectly executed forward play in classic Victorian style. He never missed the ball and he broke the bowlers' hearts.

Jack and Glenn Radford, the Australian brothers, attended Spring Hill and, whilst at School, they received letters from their idol, the great Australian batsman, Don Bradman.

> *Dear Jack,*
> *Your mother tells me you and Glenn are very keen cricket enthusiasts. I sincerely hope you keep your love fro cricket always for it is the greatest of games and even if one does not excel, a pleasure to play, Best wishes for your future success, Yours Sincerely,*
> *Don Bradman.*

> *Dear Glenn,*
> *I believe you, like Jack, are very fond of cricket. You should be able to help one another quite a lot being together at school. Learn first to have a good defence but don't be afraid to hit the ball. Very best wishes, Sincerely yours, Don Bradman.*

For practice junior boys had to walk to the Racecourse, but seniors cycled there. In the mid 1930s, a welcome change was that:-

We have a motor bus to take us to and bring us back from the Racecourse where we play cricket three times a week. It is better for both big and little boys. The little boys do not have the tiring walks before and after cricket as they did previously and the big boys are spared the ride through the streets which have more traffic every year.

**The Cricketing Brothers,
Lyonel & Kenneth Pritchard, 1931**
Courtesy of D. Pritchard

**The Radford Brothers,
Glenn and Jack**
Courtesy of D. Pritchard

Jack Attwood

Jack Murphy

School Cricket Team, 1930
Standing: Noel Maltass (Scorer), Kenneth Pritchard, Dick Murphy, Philip Gibbons, Henry Wallbright, Freddy Davey
Sitting: Jack Hill, Bernard Pitcher, Mr. Mundin, Mr. Ince-Jones, Lyonel Pritchard, Saville Wallace
Courtesy of P. Gibbons

Old boys setting out to field

Tennis

Mrs. Attwood and Jack Attwood gave a large silver cup for tennis and the winner of the tennis tournament received a replica of the Attwood Cup presented by Mr. Ince-Jones. Tournaments were arranged for Seniors and Juniors and played on the lawn tennis court at Spring Hill. To give an idea of the playing standards, Jack Murphy (1917 – 1928) reached the semi-final of the All-Ireland Junior Tennis Championship in 1930. In 1932 Kenneth Pritchard won the Attwood Tennis Cup.

Swimming

Mr. Mundin was responsible for instructing boys to swim and the swimming bath was at Midsummer Meadow, south of Spring Hill. Practically every boy at Spring Hill could swim. In 1928 Mr. Ince-Jones donated two silver cups for swimming and then in 1930 the parents of Christopher Ham presented two silver cups annually for swimming as long as Christopher was at school. The cups were always on show on the mantelpiece in the Dining Room at Spring Hill.

In 1931 nine out of ten boys were successful in gaining the Northampton Life Saving Society's Certificates. Jack Radford, the best all round swimmer, just failed to win the men's 220 yards certificate by swimming the distance in 4 minutes. However he came out an easy first in swimming competitions.

In May 1932 the rainfall was over six inches.

Extensive floods occurred in the Nene Valley and rose to the highest point we have ever seen. We were amused to see only the seats and boxes standing above the water in our swimming baths!

The bath was so small, about 21 yards by 10 yards, that the boys taking the quarter of a mile certificate had to swim 21 lengths. Two years later the swimming baths had warm water flowing in from the electric power station. The partition between the men's and women's baths was removed, thus introducing for the first time the mixed bathing in one large bath. Half of the bath was shallow and reserved for non-swimmers. A new set of diving boards was added.

Indoor Swimming Baths, Midsummer Meadow

The Arnold Way

Boys mowing the lawn tennis court, 1931.
Courtesy of P. Gibbons

Above:
Boys putting on the Spring Hill lawn, 1930

Diving at Swimming Baths, Midsummer Meadow

Football

Good football with such small numbers of varying ages would have been out of the question, but during the early 1910s the footballers from Spring Hill joined forces with another school, Eaglehurst College, and matches were played against other local schools.

The boys had good coaches from the representatives of the Football Association for Schools and from first class professional footballers, including the famous International, "Fanny" Walden. Their quick eyes enabled them to pick up the essentials, though they could never hear the agonised shouts of "Pass"!

During the mid-thirties, instead of walking or cycling to Abington Park for football on Monday afternoons, a motor bus was used to take and bring the teams back. Mr. Ince-Jones bought each of the team a jersey with green and white vertical stripes. One side wore them while the other wore white shirts so that two teams could be distinguished easily when they played against each other.

The School Football team's regular opponents were the Eaglehurst College team. After a home match win of 3 -1, the School team played away at the Racecourse in March 1937. Christopher Ham's report read:-

Before the game we were afraid we should have snow. We had had two heavy showers since dinner. Fortunately it cleared up. We all changed in the gentlemen's dressing room at the Racecourse Pavilion. Christopher Ham won the toss and decided to play against the wind.
When we started, the game was rather ragged. Bill Jenkins scored first with a shot from very close range. Presently Eaglehurst equalised with a very good goal. After a short time, Bill made a fine run and centred to Bobby Voss, who scored a second. After ten minutes Neville Coughlan scored a third when we rushed their goal.

Back Row: P. Melvin, G. Street, D. Thomas, J. Wright, T. Adams, G. Knowles
Front Row: R. Webb, R. Voss, C. Ham, W. Jenkins, G. Fair
Spring Hill Magazine ,1938

The Arnold Way

During the interval we had slices of lemon, which were refreshing after a hard game.
In the second half both sides played much better. There was more combination and both teams scored twice... when the final whistle blew, the score was 5 – 3 in our favour. We returned to the gentlemen's room where we made good use of the wash-basins and foot-baths. It was a new experience for us. Both teams and our juniors were entertained to a delicious tea by Mr. Ince-Jones.

Cross-Country Running,

The Spring Hill School combined with a hearing school for a few years for a Sports Day; but it did not work out very well. So cross-country running was introduced and became a regular annual sporting event.

In 1922 Mr. Ince-Jones donated two silver cups for annual cross-country running championships. A programme of cross-country running was set and for training the boys had a number of runs. The course ran along the Billing Road, through the fields towards the Old Mill, down Rushmere Road and back along the Bedford Road to the finish at Spring Hill. The length was about four and a half miles. All boys entered for the competition and had their own handicap times.

In 1932 Philip Lewis came first, having completed the course in 30 minutes and 39 seconds, and won the Scratch Cross Country Cup and Neville Coughlan won the Handicap Cup.

The photograph of the start of the cross-country running (1936) shows the western side of Spring Hill House. Christopher Ham wrote:-

This year we began our practice runs in good time and had a number before the final race. The course was the same as usual, about four miles long. On the last Wednesday of the term we had the final race for the cups presented by Mr. and Mrs. Ince Jones. We were started off according to our handicaps, Georges Salomon, the youngest runner starting six minutes before Alistair Fisher and Philip Lewis who were scratch. The handicap was one minute per year below the age of 19 years. Fourteen boys ran.

Cross-Country Running, 1936 —*Start of the run*

The Arnold Way

A cycle ride, 1931
Courtesy of P. Gibbons

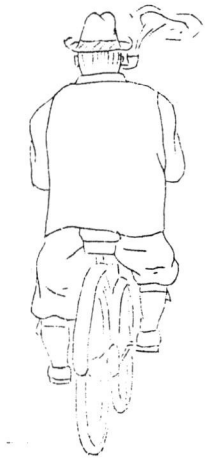

Mʀ INCE-JONES.

Cycling

Cycling trips were always arranged over the half term periods. One of the cycling trips was the visit to Althorp Park in 1936. An account written by one of the riders described the trip:-

It must have warmed the cockles of the headmaster's heart to see so many boys nice and clean in their second-best suits and very best boots. Mrs. Ince-Jones also accompanied us on her bicycle. We left our bicycles in the fine Georgian stables and were shown round by the head gardener ... After seeing the formal gardens – the close-cut box hedges and rose-garden where the library once stood – we came upon a lake with a boat on it. Mr. Ince-Jones, Alistair Fisher and Bobby Voss got in, and went for a joy-ride. Almost immediately they got stuck in the weeds, but after much violent rocking of the boat, they got clear, and the distressed British seamen returned safely to land! Then we saw the dairies and the deer. A few minutes' walk brought us to the kitchen gardens where we saw one of the finest herbaceous borders we have ever seen, and walked through what seemed to be miles of hot-houses. We saw peaches, nectarines and melons growing, and also a hot-house full of carnations of different colours.

Althorp House

Lord Spencer had promised to show us round his picture gallery if he had been at home, but unfortunately he was away, and we did not see it. After our truly enjoyable visit, we had tea at the Fox and Hounds at Harlestone.

David (John) Wright enjoyed his cycle rides and wrote:-

For cycling trips, Mr. Ince-Jones would lead the boys out, the youngest behind him and the seniors at the back. He would wear a suit of light blue plus-fours, khaki raincoat, and old soft trilby hat with his black briar pipe. The rides were not more than 20 miles in the afternoon. He rode an ancient and singular bicycle, high saddled.

We also enjoyed an interesting ride to Harpole. At first we had to ride against a strong wind but afterwards it was better going. We were interested in the gargoyles in the church, and some of us made unkind comparisons

Blackberry picking

Blackberry picking was a popular autumnal tradition which started from Mr. Dixon's days. For example, in 1931, as a result of a competition, a total of 77 lbs of blackberries were gathered, a record for Spring Hill so far. Saville Wallace was the champion picker with six and a half lbs.

Walking along the Blisworth Canal

The following year saw a new award called the *Knight of the Blackberry* and it went to Bobby Voss who broke records for the heaviest weight of collected blackberries and he was the champion for five years running. The most *Sir* Bobby Voss could collect was nine and a quarter lbs. and at the same time the total collected by the boys reached one hundred lbs. which was another new record! From these expeditions, blackberry jam made by Mrs. Ince-Jones was always a feature on the table for high tea.

To obtain blackberries, during October, boys *dropped their books on the floor and were armed with baskets*. They went to the railway station and caught the train for Roade. Then they walked to Plain Woods and then for one and half hours, they collected as many blackberries as they could pick. After that they walked back with heavy baskets along the Blisworth Canal and had tea at Blisworth Hotel. Finally they returned by train. On arrival at School, their blackberries were weighed and the boys wrote weights on the blackboard to ascertain which boy had the most weight.

Bee-Keeping

Mr. Ince-Jones thought about starting bee-keeping for some time as a possible and useful venture for the boys, perhaps part of his beloved Botany course, to promote pollination in the garden. So in 1935 he bought a new bee hive. From this hive, a plan of its construction was drawn and from this, several new bee hives were made in the workshop. These finished products were given three coats of white lead paint.

Senior boys made a bee hive

Mr. Swann, the Hon. Secretary of the Northamptonshire Bee-keepers' Association, came with a swarm of bees. The boys gathered round with great interest and watched how he inserted the bees into the hive. Once the operation was carried out, Mr. Swann came every few weeks to examine the hive and showed the boys what to do. By July, about fifty lbs of honey was collected. It was a profitable business for the School, another item on the table for high tea.

One Saturday in 1936 Bill Jenkins spotted a swarm of bees settling at the top of the old apple-tree. Alarm was raised and Mr. Ince-Jones rushed for Mr. Swann, who came immediately to deal with the swarm. The boys were curious about the bees: were they their own bees or strangers? Mr. Swann explained that the bees belonged to Spring Hill by law because they were not followed by anyone. After Mr. Swann's climb up by ladder, the smoked swarm was taken off and shaken into the skep. Mr. Swann then examined the hive and found two empty queen bee cells, thus deducing that the swarm had probably originated from the said hive. It was a very constructive lesson for the boys. The practice of bee-keeping continued up to the end of World War Two.

Mr. Swann
Courtesy of Local History Studies,
Northampton

The Arnold Way

Winter Scenes

Lyonel Pritchard
Courtesy of D. Pritchard

Kenneth Pritchard
Courtesy of D. Pritchard

Ice-Skaters.
Richard Murphy, [French mistress] and Bernard Pitcher
Courtesy of D. Pritchard

Outings

Coach Outing
Courtesy of D. Pritchard

Staff having their lunch.
Mr. Ince-Jones, Mrs. Ince-Jones, Miss Sandford (teacher), The French mistress, and Mr. Mundin
Courtesy of D. Pritchard

The Arnold Way

Outings

Boys having their lunch
Courtesy of D. Pritchard

Freddy Davey, cartoonist
Spurs Deaf Chronicle

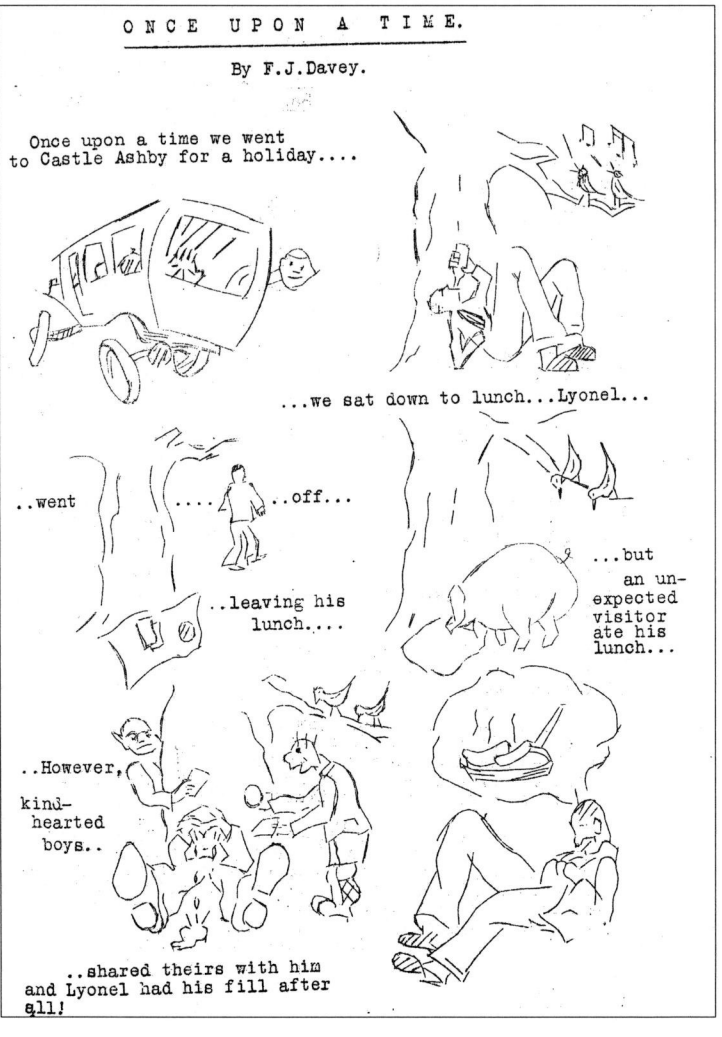

Outings

Enjoying their stroll, 1927
Jack Attwood (behind), Jack Hill, Stanley Powell, Kenneth Pritchard and Jack Murphy
Courtesy of P. Gibbons

On the left side of an inn, Richard Murphy and Lyonel Pritchard resting on the bench
Courtesy of D. Pritchard

Outings

An unidentified boy wrote:

Following a track to Maidwell Dale, we came across some farm-labourers shearing sheep. One of them was clipping off the wool by hand and another was using a machine. Most of us expected the sheep to be fidgety but they were quiet and docile. Many of us took photographs of the scene.

Sheep-shearing. One of the Spring Hill boys took a sample of sheep's wool for the lesson.
Courtesy of Philip Gibbons

In the Dale beside the lake we consumed our sandwiches. Our joy was great when Mr. Ince-Jones handed us each a bottle of lemonade or ginger-beer according to our fancy. Then the older boys had a botany talk with Mr. Ince-Jones while the juniors explored the dale with Mr. Mundin and found the source of a Nene tributary. And all this while, the ladies had "forty winks".

A meet of the Pytchley Hunt at Flaxton, attended by Spring Hill boys in the autumn of 1932
Spring Hill Magazine, 1932

POPULAR SCHOOL OUTINGS

A motor coach ready to take boys out
Courtesy of P. Gibbons

OUTSIDE SHAKESPEARE'S BIRTHPLACE.

After reading some Shakespearean plays, the School party visited Stratford on Avon by motor coach and watched a Shakespearean performance. Such visits helped some of the boys who took English Literature including a selected Shakespearean play in their Oxford School Certificate examinations.

POPULAR SCHOOL OUTINGS

(Valentine's Series Postcard)

The visit to the Gunpowder Plot Room, Ashby St. Ledgers and the annual fireworks display and the burning of the Guy Fawkes bonfire was a regular event in November at Spring Hill.

(Abington Park Series)

Chapter 6

The Finale

Mr. C. G. Goodwin, the Vice-President of the National College of Teachers of the Deaf, spent a month at Spring Hill as a substitute teacher for the absent Mr. Mundin in May 1939. He thought that

... the nature of the work itself, the curriculum, including literature, science and mathematics, indicated the high standard attained by the pupils. By means of the Socratic method, the training and testing questions lead the pupil to think and discover for himself, and while much was expected of him, there was no lack of encouragement to stimulate his efforts. Individual instruction was a regular feature of the work in all subjects and carried out as it is throughout the school, each pupil at his particular stage of learning reflected its value. The evening preparation time revealed to me the earnestness of the boys in a desire to fix acquired truths. They also took the opportunity to seek to overcome some difficulty they had met with during the day. I was very favourably impressed with the quality of speech of the boys and with their ability to lipread. The use of colloquial language was fluent and it became a pleasure to hold conversations with them.

An extract from the minutes of the NCTD Executive meeting in June 1939 reads:-

Mr. Ince-Jones, apologising for the absence of Mr. Goodwin, remarked how, in his usual self-effacing manner, Mr. Goodwin at very short notice had come to his aid and had rendered invaluable assistance during a difficult period and had succeeded in making himself popular with all at Northampton.

Based on the School language teaching scheme, which was tried out and improvised since the 1920s, both Mr. Ince-Jones and Mr. Mundin always stimulated and kept interest by basing language teaching on the boys' own activities and by providing constantly varying experiences. These language lessons were invaluable because deaf boys gained first hand experiences and facts which they wanted to ask and to talk about.

For example, it was around 1939 that Mr. Mundin and his junior boys explored Northampton in a variety of ways. Text books about the town were not used. The boys were encouraged to write their own book called "My Book of Northampton". As each lesson proceeded, a blackboard summary was built up and at the end of the lesson copied in their special book. The boys took pride in their books and improved their writing and illustrations week by week. In the evening following the lesson, their "prep" or homework lasted for about 45 minutes under supervision and consisted of either studying the summary or writing answers to questions on the lesson. The following morning five minutes were spent in oral questioning to ensure that the work had been done satisfactorily. Thus the work proceeded until just before the end of the term when a lesson was spent in revision of the term's work, prior to a written test.

The School bank, which Mr. Ince-Jones ran since 1935, was another language activity. Each boy had his own cheque book, paying-in book and pass-book, and kept his own personal accounts. Money was paid into the bank at the beginning of each term, and the boys were allowed to withdraw money by cheque when the School bank was open one morning in the week. From the School bank to branches of the National Banks in the town was the next step.

Frequent School Industrial Visits

The famous Barratt's boot and shoe-making firm was a favourite visit. Its building is opposite 21 Primrose Hill where the Northampton School for the Deaf was established in 1868.

The Clicking Room — Messrs. Barratt's.

Morris Motor car industry, Cowley, Oxford

Northampton Gasworks

The blocks for the Spring Hill Magazine were made at Clark and Sherwells' printing firm

David Hyslop (1937 – 1945) commented that during his time at Spring Hill School some boys came from abroad, for example,

David Hyslop
Spurs Deaf Chronicle

Bobby Voss and John Wright, later famed for his poetry writing were from South Africa while the Wilson twins, Alan and David, were from New Zealand. Of the boys, he knew Philip Melvin whose father was a noted musician and stage comedian, often partnering George Robey. George Street earned the distinction of being the first boy in school with his portable hearing aid. Philip Lewis stayed at school till the age of 23! Bill Jenkins, being an outstanding sportsman, excelled at both football and cricket. After he left school, he played cricket professionally. John Napier was the descendant from General Napier famed for his military services in India.

David's best teacher in his life was Mr. F. Ince-Jones. Today David Hyslop from Shirley, Birmingham, is an OBE award holder for his long services to Breakthrough Trust, which promotes the integration of deaf and hearing people.

Mr. G. S. Melvin, Philip Melvin and Mr. Ince-Jones
Spring Hill School Magazine

George Drewry's account of his years (1939 – 1945) gives an outline of the activities of Spring Hill School during the Second World War:

Looking back into the mists of time, it requires time for reflection undistracted by the minutiae of present everyday living to recapture in my mind's eye the pattern of my school life at Spring Hill, Northampton. For me, it was a dual experience in that my induction into what was my first residential school at the tender age of 8 more or less coincided with the opening of hostilities between Great Britain and Germany in 1939. My deaf parents, suitably impressed by the outgoing personality of an athlete-looking lad of 14 by name of David Hyslop, left me and my 6 year old brother [Ralph R. Drewry] behind with a strong reassurance that David would keep an eye on us.

George Drewry

War-time school life centred on the Big School Room and Little School Room in an outbuilding bordering a stable yard in an area to the left of a generous circular one-way drive that set back from Cliftonville Road a large Victorian town house of ample proportions with a grass tennis court on the right and a kitchen garden at the back, all within a high walled garden.

The Arnold Way

George and Ralph Drewry on the way to School with their mother. May 1942
Courtesy of George Drewry

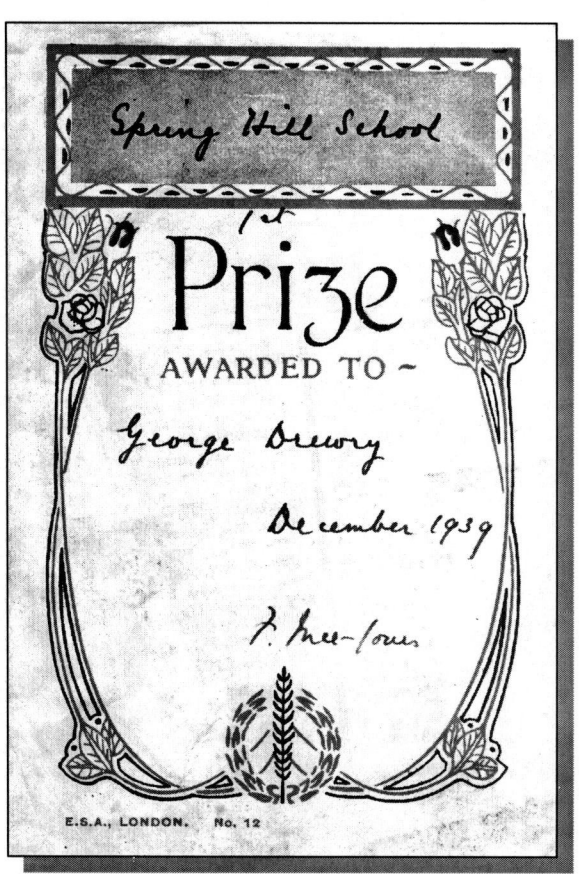

George Drewry's Prize Certificate, 1939

Meals were taken in an oak-panelled dining room. Mr. Ince-Jones, the owner-headmaster, presided at the end of a large table flanked by his wife and two teenage daughters while the matron dished out war-time fare at the other end. Each Monday morning the boys anxiously gathered around a duty prefect as he posted a revised seating plan to find out which six of them had to sit at the head's table while the rest of the 22 boys were distributed over the second large table and two small side-tables. There was, of course, more spontaneous conversation away from the head's table though one or two seniors confident in speech and steeped in knowledge of botany sought every opportunity to discuss the mysterious intricacies of whorls and stamens with Mr. Ince-Jones. However, lack of fluency in speech and language did not deter those who fancied their chances of sitting next to or opposite Pamela the younger of the two daughters of the head.

The ethos of good table manners and table talk introduced at the founding of this school for the "Sons of Gentlemen" was somewhat spoilt by the fact that the duty prefect stamped on the thin hollow floorboards of the Big Schoolroom to summon us to carry our school chairs to the dining room each mealtime (not that it did us any harm!)

A typical school day started with a douche in cold water. More often than not we got our feet wet on account of any one of us missing our target during our nocturnal trips to the chamber pot housed beneath the wash basin! Wheatabix or shredded wheat (fried rashers, etc. on Sundays), followed by toast, set us up for morning school.

Assembly was a ritualistic affair with us standing in rows facing a Honours board at one end of the Big Schoolroom waiting for the familiar vibrations of the head's measured footsteps approaching from behind. I made use of any delay in his otherwise punctual schedule to study the names on the Honours board. The painstakingly hand-scribed names of those long gone old boys conjured up fantasies in my mind. Of those who distinguished themselves in external matriculation examinations, two stick in my mind. One was David Wright who, as a freshman, cycled over from Oxford University to visit us and later became a distinguished poet. The other whom I came to know in later life was Dr. Bernard Pitcher who studied geology at London University. The prayers lasted a few minutes with the head reading aloud from a well-worn prayer card and the boys and Staff reciting (or mumbling as the case might have been) words simultaneously.

Prayers over and done with, we stood in our form groups in front of the blackboard that ran the length of the big Schoolroom for news of the day. When I was in the third form, Mr. Mundin the senior master, read extracts from the Daily Telegraph for us to discuss. Every opportunity was taken to introduce us to new vocabulary and correct our English usage and pronunciation. Naturally the war topics captured our interest but we were frustrated by the constant corrections. The graphic sketch maps of the active war frontline alarmed us when black arrows showed panzer gains and elated us when white arrows showed encircling Allied counter attacks.

Then came the welcome 11 o'clock break with a hurried gulp of our daily half pint ration of milk prior to a football kick-about with a much mutilated tennis ball on the cobbled surface of the high walled stable yard.

The rest of morning school was, I recall, devoted to the core subjects such as English, Geography and History. The minutes ticked away too slowly for our young growing bodies which craved for the succour that lunch-time promised. Our attention tended to wander, but indulgence in day-dreaming had its own perils. The Geography master, himself no mean cricketer, often swivelled from the blackboard to hurl his piece of chalk at a luckless boy's forehead with deadly accuracy. However, after being repeatedly targeted with consequential smarting pain, the serial offender hatched a bright idea. Alerted, his peers waited with bated breath as he deliberately made hand gestures behind the master's back. Sure enough, within seconds, the anticipated "exocet" was on its way, locked on target only to be deflected upwards by the intended victim's perfectly timed lifting of his hinged desk top!

The first afternoon session was spent on composition writing or class reading of stories from Shakespeare or Aesop's Fables. Those of us, who had reasonable facility in English and lipreading, got by. But the real test of our diligence, or lack of it, came in a fusillade of questions from the head -woe betided those of us who had skipped or even skimmed our prep (homework). Occasionally the persistent transgressors found they couldn't sit down after a visit to the head's study – the head's dreaded command, "come to the study", was usually enough to keep most of us on the "straight and narrow"! Fortunately, all was not gloom and doom, as the head, himself a fine story teller and actor, had a gift for bringing Shakespeare to life. I vividly remember him, a portly man with baggy "plus-fours" and a monocle, prancing around as Malvolio with yellow stockings in the play Twelfth Night – that was some sixty years ago!

The head and senior master shared the teaching of the scriptures. Also there was a bible class for the seniors on Sunday evenings.

For outdoor pursuits, we let off steam on Monday afternoons during drill. Divided into four teams, Pirates, Rovers, Skyhawks and Crusaders, we went through various uninspiring exercise routines till the last 5 – 10 minutes when we had competitive team games such as "twos and threes".

Tuesdays and Fridays saw us changing into our football gear and marching eagerly downhill to Midsummer Meadow. In wet weather, we occasionally found the pitch unplayable

The Arnold Way

because of the high water-table, the flood meadow being next to the River Nene. Around the pitch the meadow was studded with 'v' shaped steel bars of heavy section inverted and let into the ground as barriers against possible use of the meadow as landing ground by German troop-carrying gliders.

Matches were organised between the four drill teams with changing permutations of any two of them joining forces against the other two. Mr. Mundin was the regular referee and used his A.R.P. whistle and a persil-white handkerchief which he flagged to attract our attention. The return uphill trudge to school was hard on our weary legs and this was often compounded as stud nails were pushed through our football boot soles by the rapid wearing down of the leather studs on tarmac.

It was on the Northampton Racecourse that we played cricket. To get there we travelled in a double-decker bus with the upper half of windows stained dark blue to dim the lights from observation by German bombers flying overhead en route to cities such as Coventry and Liverpool to deliver their deadly cargoes. We, juniors, had a great incentive to try and join the senior squad who received expert coaching from 'Fanny' Waldon, a retired ex-Spurs footballer and ex-Northants cricketer.

Weeding time in the Spring Hill garden, July 1942
L to R: John Hadfield, Denis Forbes, John Wingrove, Mr.Ince-Jones, Kevin Perry, David Hyslop, Michael Sutton, Peter King (near greenhouse), Michael Strong, Barry Haycox.
Courtesy of George Drewry

Friday lunch-time was pocket money time and the head left the dining room to fetch a bank sealed envelope containing 40 silver sixpence coins. On his return, he moved down the lines of boys seated at tables and placed a sixpence piece on each boy's side plate, extracting a "thank you, sir" from each boy before moving onto the next one. My brother and I were the odd ones as we received a brass threepenny coin each.

Garden work occupied us on Saturday mornings. Seniors were allocated parcels of the kitchen garden to cultivate or otherwise maintain as their contribution to the "Dig for Victory" campaign and juniors found it was a lottery as to whether they helped an easy-going senior who appreciated their input or an over-zealous senior who kept his assistants toiling longer! We

added greatly to the quantity and variety of food on table. The head's wife looked after two bee-hives. Fruit-picking was seen as sport by those of us who loved the thrill of climbing up to the outermost branches of trees and shaking them to send apples or pears raining down. Most were caught before hitting the ground. Thus we ate fruit in season but surplus fruit were bottled for winter use.

Sundays had us, juniors, struggling with studs fastening our starched Eton collars to our shirts. This was a part of our Sunday attire consisting of navy blue jackets and shorts and gleaming black Oxford shoes. We never liked parading in crocodile formation along the streets to All Saints' Church with plain green caps (plain grey felt hats with floppy brims in summer). We, juniors, sat in a gallery at the back of the nave. The morning service was always an interminable purgatory, none of my peer group being able to follow, let alone understand, it. At best, we were drilled into going through motions, standing up and sitting down on cue and when we knelt down for long periods, our knees ached.

The service at last ended with organ music giving way to loud rumbles in our tummies, we marched back to school, not forgetting our gasmasks in rectangular government issued cardboard boxes that accompanied us everywhere. Interestingly, the head and his family promenaded on the other side of the road from us. The Sunday roast had to wait till after we had brought our letters home to the head for vetting and posting (we learnt to write carefully in time-honoured formats to avoid unsolicited lessons in composition and spelling!)

The highlights of the school term were few and far between but when they happened, we appreciated them all the more. They usually fell at half-term, which lasted only one day.

The last great event of the year was the annual Christmas party. It was preceded by a ritual performed during lunch towards the end of November. Boys took turns to walk up to a side table, solemnly take up a wooden spoon and stir the Christmas pudding ingredients in a large galvanised laundry basket, saying at the same time "I wish happy Christmas to everyone in this house". This ritual begot another – that of counting off the number of remaining days of the term on the billiard marker board by whoever reached the dining room first for breakfast each morning!

The Christmas party traditionally kicked off with a superb treasure hunt in the head's private suite and gave us the rare opportunity to satisfy our morbid curiosity as to where exactly the canes (a selection of them, we were told) were kept in the study. This was followed by the annual prize-giving in the Drawing Room and the arrival of Father Christmas via the storey-high sash window. As far as we were concerned, it was an authentic Santa; somehow we didn't question the obvious absence of the head from our midst!

The eventual dinner was capped by the ceremonial carrying in of the Christmas pudding covered in bluish flames – a magic ritual culminating in our search for sixpence pieces in the pudding. Finally we trooped over to the big schoolroom for the boisterous dance, Sir Roger de Coverly, before retiring to bed a good three hours after normal bedtime. Such was life at Spring Hill as seen from a junior's perspective.

The war seemed remote but there were constant reminders of it. Occasional air raid warnings sent us to sleep in the cellar.

Meanwhile, behind closed doors in 1942 Mr. Ince-Jones applied to the Board of Education to have his private school recognised by the government in view of his pupils' successes in the past. As a result, two inspectors of schools, Mrs. Parkes and Mr. Lumsden,

The Arnold Way

The last School Group, photographed in July 1942

Back Row: D. Hyslop, K. Perry, D. Forbes, M. Gent, M. Messer, M. Strong, J. Wingrove, M. Sutton, W. Adams. A. Morris
Middle Row: Pamela Ince-Jones, B. Goode, G.Evans, Mrs. Mundin, Mr. Mundin, Mrs. Ince-Jones, Mr. Ince-Jones, Miss Cox, Miss Milton, P. King, J. Pickworth, K. Stephens, Patrica Ince-Jones
Front Row: R. Drewry, J. Scott, G. Drewry, S. Barkes, W. Clay, G. Munro, B. Haycox, J. Hadfield

visited the school on February 18 1943. They thought that the Spring Hill premises were well maintained in view of the war restrictions of the use of labour and materials. The dormitories were found to be sufficient for 23 boys, *and are homely, plainly but adequately furnished, and well ventilated.* There were 3 baths and 6 W.C.'s.

The annual salaries of the staff were:-

Mr. Mundin	*£420 non-resident*
Miss Milton	*£100 resident*
Mrs. Mundin	*£100 non-resident, mornings only*
Miss Martin	*£75 non-resident, 3 days a week*
Mr. Baxter	*one afternoon per week.*

The fees, including the board fee, are £50 per term, but on occasions boys specially deserving have been taken for less.

The inspectors visited all classes and noted that, owing to the wide age range and different time spent in school, no general scheme of work covering the subjects was given except for examination requirements. Mr. Lumsden later wrote an appreciation of his relation Miss J. S. Cooper, who was present amongst the staff during the inspection visit at Spring Hill:-

... I was saved from the embarrassment of having to inspect her by the headmaster's determination that I should understand that only his own work mattered...

Mr. Ince-Jones gave some particulars on ex-pupils and pointed out that a few of them could enter paid employment direct from school as the school did not provide vocational training. Many of them made good progress in occupations related to their fathers on a voluntary basis and later proved themselves worthy of a salary. Others, for example, architects, required long courses of professional training at the parents' expense. Others such as farmers and horticulturists required capital to start in business.

In the end the inspectors recommended that:-

... recognition be accorded to this school, as an efficient educational institution doing work of secondary level but of unique type since it caters only for deaf boys

whereupon the Board of Education gave its approval. An advertisement was inserted in *The Teacher of the Deaf* in order to recruit more deaf boys into Spring Hill School.

> **PRIVATE SCHOOL FOR DEAF BOYS,**
> SPRINGHILL, NORTHAMPTON.
> Boys of all ages given a thorough education by Speech and Lip-reading on Preparatory and Public School lines. Remarkable results in public examinations. Many boys prepared for professions and the Universities. Cricket, football, tennis, swimming, carpentry and all the advantages of normal school life with pleasant home atmosphere. Highly qualified staff. Individual attention. Modern hearing aids in constant use.
> Apply for prospectus to:—Headmaster, F. Ince-Jones, B.Sc., Barrister-at-Law.

During the summer vacation of 1943, Mr. Ince-Jones, who had been ill for nearly a year, was admitted to the local hospital for an operation. He was advised to have at least two months of complete rest, but in the interests of his School he defied his doctors and returned to work after five weeks in hospital with the wounds still unhealed.

The year 1944 was Mr. Ince-Jones's *annus miserabilis*. He felt weak and could not play his customary cricket matches with the boys. Mr. Mundin felt burdened in taking on extra teaching tasks for the ailing Mr. Ince-Jones and, having felt the strain for so long, he decided to apply for the post of Senior Master at the Northern Counties School for the Deaf in Newcastle. He gave Mr. Ince-Jones three months' notice when his application was accepted.

> **HIGH SCHOOL FOR DEAF BOYS, NORTHAMPTON.**
>
> Wanted urgently in September, Assistant (Lady or Gentleman). Apply at once to F. Ince-Jones, Spring Hill, Cliftonville, Northampton.

An advertisement for the vacant post was inserted in *The Teacher of the Deaf* for April 1944, but to no avail. Another one was inserted in June 1944 and again no response. So Mr. Ince-Jones had to resort to local teachers for help.

> **HIGH SCHOOL FOR DEAF BOYS, SPRING HILL, NORTHAMPTON.**
> (Recognised by the Board of Education).
>
> WANTED in September, qualified assistant master, degree desirable. Salary up to £400, according to qualifications and experience. Reserved occupation. Apply to F. Ince-Jones, Headmaster.

The death of Mr. Hugh Neville Dixon took place at his home, 17 St. Matthew's Parade, Northampton, on May 9 1944 at the age of 83 years. His wife, Mary, died just five months before him on December 27 1943. The funeral service was held at Doddridge Congregational Church where Mr. Dixon gave service for 59 years and was a life deacon. A memorial plaque was placed inside on one side of the church walls.

On May 14 1944 Abraham Farrar, the Grand Old Boy of the Northampton High School for the Deaf, passed away at the age of 83. The closeness of the two deaths of such prominent people in the School history and the loss of his *valued* teacher, Mr. Mundin, seemed to have affected Mr. Ince-Jones badly.

George Drewry continued:-

Following the D-Day landings, the Allied forces were starting to drive the German armies out of Normandy when a fortnight before Spring Hill was due to break up for the 1944 summer vacation, we were all stunned by a shock announcement that Mr. Ince-Jones had been taken ill and so the school would close forthwith, never to re-open. It was the end of an unrivalled era in deaf education over which Mr. Ince-Jones had presided as owner-headmaster for some 40 years. For some of the 22 boys, it was the end of their school career and they had to look for work once they got home. My brother (11) and I (13) stayed at home while our parents searched frantically for alternative placements for us.

I have been asked why the capable Mr. Mundin, the school's long serving senior master, did not take over the school or, at least, keep it running for a while. It appeared to me that the answer was a simple one – it was that the ownership of the school was vested in Mr. Ince-Jones and Mr. Mundin was not in a position financially to take over.

Mr. Ince-Jones thought *the staff both for teaching and domestic work was hopelessly inadequate*, and announced the closure of his School.

However, a change of mind led Mr. Ince-Jones to write a letter to the Secretary of the Board of Education on July 31 1944. It read:-

> *This is to tell you and the Board of Education that within the last few days I have decided to try to carry on my school for deaf boys with much fewer pupils, not more than seven or eight for the present. In this way we shall preserve a nucleus and possibly build up later if conditions render this practicable.*
>
> *We shall have a small School Certificate class and a small class of bright junior boys doing semi-secondary work.*
>
> *My wife and I are in better health than we were at the end of last term and, though we could not attempt, with the present inadequate help, to cope with the full school, we believe we can mange the smaller number. The doctors have given us permission to try.*
>
> *We are doing this in response to pathetic appeals, in the hope of being of some service to deaf boys. These boys have nothing suitable to which to go. We hope to hold on at any rate until better times give some reasonable alternatives.*
>
> *I realise that the school, though retaining all essentials, will be much smaller than before but hope the Board will see its way in the special circumstances to continue its recognition.*

Courtesy of the National Archives, Kew (Ref 33/137)

One of his earliest ex-pupils, Noel Brunning-Maddison, offered his help but Mr. Ince-Jones declined his offer as he seemed to have recovered well enough to give all the Science teaching required.

George Drewry carried on with his account of schooldays :-

However in December 1944 Mr. Ince-Jones felt well enough to consider re-opening of the school for eight boys only and fortunately my brother and I were amongst those invited to return. Also offered places were Graeme Munro, Sharer Barkes, John Hadfield, Dennis Forbes and David Hyslop.

Ginger the School cat died in the early Spring of 1945 at the age of 14 years, the pride and glory of Spring Hill. Miss Patricia Ince-Jones wrote:-

During the summer months when the [Ince-Jones] family were on holiday, he could not bear to be parted from Spring Hill and when adopted by friends he would invariably return and be found none the worse for his cross-country journey through Northampton, basking in the sun at Spring Hill. During his fourteen years Ginger by many endearing habits and ways became popular with those who knew him. He is buried in the garden he loved.

Ginger, the School cat

The cessation of the war in Europe was marked by a Victory in Europe day on May 8 1945.

The school had barely re-opened for the summer term 1945 when within a week or two we celebrated V.E. day with Mr. Ince-Jones' family at their country cottage in Harpole. By the end of the day Mr. Ince-Jones was taken ill again. His wife had no alternative but to ask us to go home the next morning. We never returned as the school had closed for the last time.

May 9 1945 was the official date of the closure of the Northampton High School for Deaf Boys.

Mr. & Mrs. Mundin

At conferences and meetings where teachers of the deaf gathered together to give talks on issues linked with the education of the deaf or to share their experiences, Mr. Ince-Jones was always confident and was highly respected by his colleagues, but was never on intimate terms with them. He was a very private person and was a somewhat enigmatical figure, but his interests were wide and indicative of his great talents. Had he not chosen to be a teacher of the deaf he would have undoubtedly achieved high success at the Bar or in Parliament. Ever since Mr. Ince-Jones gave his speech on higher education of the deaf at the International Conference of Teachers of the Deaf held at Edinburgh in 1907, he had eleven successes in the School Certificate examinations, made more difficult in those days when it included a compulsory foreign language subject. Six boys proceeded to universities and gained degrees or diplomas. A few others gained professional qualifications as architects, accountants, missioners with the deaf, farmers, horticulturists, engineers and so on. No other schools for the deaf, whether private or not, could match such academical achievements as those at Spring Hill School. Truly a milestone in British Deaf history. These successes paved the way to the establishment of the first national public grammar school for the deaf in the United Kingdom, namely, Mary Hare Grammar School for the Deaf (MHGS), which opened in January 1946.

When Mr. Mundin became the first Principal of MHGS, he and the four ex-Springhillian pupils, who were amongst the first entrants of MHGS, namely, George and Ralph Drewry, Sharer Barkes and Graeme Munro, carried on some of the traditions of Spring Hill School to MHGS. It can be said that he was trained in order to see the essential and comprehensive contribution played in the establishment of MHGS by the Northampton School.

George Drewry *Sharer Barkes* *Ralph Drewry* *Graeme Munro*

Mr. Ince Jones had by April 1946 recovered fully from ill-health after a holiday in Devon. The Spring Hill premises were up for sale, and a year later it was purchased for £8000 by the Northampton High School for Girls to set up its preparatory school for girls. Miss Patricia Ince-Jones, who became a teacher of music, joined the staff at Spring Hill in 1950. She remained there for 20 years until she fell ill and sadly died in 1975. Her younger sister, Pamela, attended the Cheltenham Ladies College, passed the School Certificate and gained Matriculation in July 1944 and settled in London.

The residence of the Ince-Jones family was at Apple Tree Cottage, High Street in Harpole, an attractive village five miles west of Northampton Town. It is a yellow sandstone cottage of two stories high and is more than three centuries old. Sitting outside in his small back garden, Mr. Frederick Ince-Jones, the last Head of the Northampton Private High School for the Deaf, would look back on his contribution to the education of the deaf with pride. Whenever Old Boys visited Harpole, he and his wife would entertain them with tea and recall many happy moments with them at Spring Hill. On February 6 1954 he died at the age of 70 after a long illness at his home. His wife, Mrs. Sarah Elizabeth Ince-Jones died on October 6 1982.

Mrs and Mr. Ince-Jones, Patricia and Pamela

Group of Boys with H.R.H. Prince William, Nov. 1944. Little Prince William is holding the hand of Patricia. This photograph was taken by H.R.H. The Duchess of Gloucester, just before she left for Australia

Apple Tree Cottage, Harpole. 2008

Mr. F. Ince-Jones relaxing by the sea
Courtesy of George Drewry

Last Christmas card from Mrs. Elizabeth Ince-Jones and Patricia Ince-Jones in late 1960s.
Courtesy of George Drewry

Appendix 1 *The Arnold Way*

Staff of the Northampton High School for the Deaf (1868 - 1945)

1868 - 1884   **1ˢᵗ head. The Rev. Thomas Arnold**
- Site:
  - 1868 - 1874 at 21 Primrose Hill, Northampton.
  - 1875 - 1877 at 27 St. Paul's Road, Northampton.
  - 1877 - 1884 at Fair View House, 17 Billing Street, Northampton.
- Title:
  - 1880 "Middle Class for the Deaf and Dumb"
  - 1881 "Middle Class School for the Deaf and Dumb"
  - 1884 "Oral School for the Deaf"
- Staff:
  - W. S. Bessant (1880 - 1882), Teacher.
  - H. N. Dixon (1883 - 1884), Pupil Teacher/Teacher.

1885 - 1908   **2ⁿᵈ head. Hugh Neville Dixon, M.A., F.L.S.**
- Site:
  - 1885 - 1887 at 25 St. Paul's Road, Northampton.
  - 1888 - 1908 at Wickham House, 23 East Parade Park, Northampton.
- Title: "High School for the Oral Education of the Deaf"
- Staff:
  - Mrs. Dixon (1885 - 1908), Housemother/Teacher.
  - Frederick Ince-Jones (1901 - 1908), Pupil Teacher/ Teacher.

1909 - 1945   **3ʳᵈ head. Frederick Ince-Jones, B.Sc., Barrister-at-Law.**
- Site:
  - 1909 - 1912 at 23 East Parade Park, Northampton.
  - 1912 - 1945 at Spring Hill, Cliftonville, Northampton.
- Title:
  - "High School for the Oral Education of the Deaf"
  - "Spring Hill School for the Deaf"
- Staff:

Frederick W. Illingworth (1912 - 1914)	Teacher
Horace Haycock (1914 - 1915)	Teacher
Edgar Lewis Mundin (1920 - 1944)	Pupil Teacher/Teacher
James Wilson Baxter (1912 - 1942)	p/t Art Master
Miss E. M.M.Phillips (1909 - 191_)	Matron
Miss Whiting (191_ - 192_ , 1935)	Matron
Miss Kirby (192_ - 1924)	Matron
Miss Lawrence (1924 -1927)	Matron
Miss Cox (1927 - 1931, 1941 - 1944)	Matron
Miss Agnew (1931 - 1932)	Matron.
Miss Castles (1932 - 1934)	Matron
Miss Richardson (1935 -1941)	Matron
Miss C. King (1916 - 1920)	Junior Teacher
Miss Knowles (1920 - 19__)	Junior Teacher
Miss Daniells (192_ - 1932)	Junior Teacher
Miss Rosamund Milton (1931 - 1942)	Junior/Art Teacher
Miss Whittaker (1932 - 1937)	Junior Teacher
Miss Sandiford (19__ - 19__)	Junior Teacher
Miss J. S. Cooper (1937 - 1943)	Junior Teacher
Miss Marshall (1940 - 1941)	Junior Teacher
Mrs. Elsie Mundin (1941 - 1944)	p/t Junior Teacher
Miss Monica Martin (1941 - 1943)	p/t Junior Teacher
Miss Haslam	
Mr. Linnell (1939 - 1945)	p/t Carpentry Instructor

The Arnold Way

Appendix 2

LIST OF EX-PUPILS OF THE NORTHAMPTON HIGH SCHOOL FOR THE DEAF

Surname	Names	Head	Enter Year	Left Year
Adams	Terry Boys	Ince Jones	1930	1937
Adams	Wilfred	Ince Jones	1935	1943
Allsebrook	Alan Pole	Dixon	1894	1900
Attwood	Jack	Ince Jones	1917?	1927
Ball	Ivan H.	Ince Jones		
Banks	Arnold	Ince Jones		1916
Barham	Eric	Ince Jones	1939	1940
Barkes	John Sharer	Ince Jones	1941	1945
Bilibin	Alexander	Ince Jones	1913	1921
Bottomley	George H.	Dixon		
Bowers	Frank H.	Ince Jones		
Broatch	Cyril			
Brown	C.A.	Ince Jones		
Brunning-Maddison	Noel G.	Dixon	1903	1907
Byers	Robert A.	Ince Jones		1925
Calder	Gordon	Ince Jones		
Carr	Cyril	Dixon	1885	1890
Cayley	John Oliver	Ince Jones	1917	1925
Charlton	Andrew	Ince Jones		
Cheremeteff	Serge	Ince Jones	1916	
Clay	Walter	Ince Jones	1938	1944
Coates	Wynne	Ince Jones		
Cobley	John	Ince Jones	1925	1935
Cockayne	William Arthur	Arnold	1875	
Condy	Charles H.B.	Dixon		
Cope	Herbert	Ince Jones		
Coughlan	Neville	Ince Jones	1928	1937
Cox	Ernest F.	Ince Jones	1937	1940
Cuthbertson	Alistair	Ince Jones	1936	1939
Dalmau	Tulio	Ince Jones	1927?	1930
Dalton	John	Ince Jones		1931
Davey	Frederick J.	Ince Jones	1917	1931
Denison	Donald	Ince Jones	1917?	1928
Dixon	Rollo Havee	Arnold	1874	1880
Donkin	George M. K.	Ince Jones	1944	1944
Doubleday	Stuart	Ince Jones		
Douglas-Irvine	Lucy C.	Arnold	1881	1884
Douglas-Irvine	William K.	Dixon		
Douglas-Irvine	Charlie Gordon	Dixon	1891	1901
Drewry	George T.	Ince Jones	1939	1945
Drewry	Ralph R.	Ince Jones	1939	1945
Druiffe	Sidney	Ince Jones		
Eady	Donald C.	Dixon		
Edward	Arthur	Dixon		

Appendix 2　　　　　　　　　　　　　　　　　　　　　*The Arnold Way*

LIST OF EX-PUPILS OF THE NORTHAMPTON HIGH SCHOOL FOR THE DEAF (Cont'd)

Surname	Names	Head	Enter Year	Left Year
England	Jimmy	Ince Jones	1917	1932
Evans	David	Ince Jones	1941	1944
Fair	Geoffrey	Ince Jones	1932	1938
Farrar	Abraham	Arnold	1868	1880
Fischer	Patrick H.	Ince Jones	1925?	1927
Fisher	Alistair K.C.	Ince Jones	1925	1936
Flemming	Hugh	Ince Jones	1928	1936
Forbes	Denis	Ince Jones	1936	1945
France	Cyril	Ince Jones		
Francis	Henry	Dixon		1892
Gemmell	Alistair	Ince Jones	1937	1937
Gent	Michael	Ince Jones	1939	1943
Gibbons	Philip	Ince Jones	1927?	1932
Gibbons	John Henry	Ince Jones		
Glenn	Norman	Ince Jones	1930	1937
Goode	Brian	Ince Jones	1941	1943
Goodwin	George	Ince Jones		
Gourley	Eric	Ince Jones		
Hadfield	John	Ince Jones	1939	1945
Ham	Christopher	Ince Jones	1925	1939
Hardcastle	Mary	Arnold	1881	1885
Harrison	John	Ince Jones	1931	1935
Haycox	Barry	Ince Jones	1941	1944
Hill	Jack	Ince Jones	1925?	1932
Hills	Joseph	Dixon		
Hodges	Eric J.H.	Ince Jones		1925
Hodgson	Eric A.	Ince Jones		1914
Holman	Peter	Ince Jones	1943	1944
Holt	Frederick A.	Arnold	1858	1862
Hood	Paul	Ince Jones	1939	1942
Hyslop	David Stephens	Ince Jones	1937	1945
Imray	Reggie	Ince Jones	1930	1934
Jenkins	Bill	Ince Jones	1933	1938
King	Hugh	Dixon		
King	Peter	Ince Jones	1939	1943
Kinloch	Freddie A.	Ince Jones	1916	
Knowles	E. Geoffrey	Ince Jones	1936	1939
Lambourne	Eric	Ince Jones	1931	1935
Levitt	Arthur	Arnold		
Lewis	Philip J.	Ince Jones		1939
Lyons	Douglas	Dixon		
Mackintosh	John	Ince Jones	1931	1937
Mallett	Charles Lynton	Dixon		1903
Maltass	Noel	Dixon	1925?	1931
Marshall	Michael	Ince Jones		

The Arnold Way

Appendix 2

LIST OF EX-PUPILS OF THE NORTHAMPTON HIGH SCHOOL FOR THE DEAF (Cont'd)

Surname	Names	Head	Enter Year	Left Year
Martin	Bolo Babu	Ince Jones		
McClure	Tom	Ince Jones		1925
Melvin	Philip Rodway	Ince Jones	1934	1941
Messer	William Michael	Ince Jones	1936	1944
Miller	Alexander	Arnold	1880	1882
Molyneux	Percy	Ince Jones		
Monins	Ray S. C.	Ince Jones	1944	
Morris	Allan	Ince Jones	1941	1944
Munro	Graeme	Ince Jones	1941	1945
Murphy	Richard A.	Ince Jones	1917?	1930
Murphy	Jack	Ince Jones		1928
Myers	David Maurice	Ince Jones	1943	1944
Napier	John	Ince Jones	1933	1938
Nicholls	Christopher E.			
Nolan	Richard	Ince Jones		
Paton	Gordon	Ince Jones	1925	1937
Peacocke	R. Ferguson	Ince Jones		1925
Perry	Kevin Peter	Ince Jones	1942	1943
Pickworth	John	Ince Jones	1937	1944
Pitcher	Bernard Lewis	Ince Jones	1925	1932
Powell	Stanley G.	Ince Jones	1925	1929
Pritchard	Lyonel Hanmer	Ince Jones	1917	1930
Pritchard	Kenneth Hanmer	Ince Jones	1917	1932
Proctor	G.	Ince Jones		
Radbone	Frank H.	Dixon	1891	1898
Radford	John	Ince Jones		1931
Radford	Glenn	Ince Jones		1931
Ross	Denys	Ince Jones	1938	
Salomon	Georges	Ince Jones	1933	1938
Sawdon	R.	Ince Jones		
Scott	James	Ince Jones	1939	1944
Shwer	Harry	Ince Jones		1925
Sieberman	Peter	Ince Jones	1934	1935
Skuse	Teddy	Ince Jones		
Smallman	Frederick A.	Ince Jones		1921
Stephens	Keith Oscar	Ince Jones	1942	1944
Street	George	Ince Jones	1932	1938
Strong	Michael	Ince Jones	1938	1943
Sutton	Michael	Ince Jones	1938	1945
Talmadge	George	Ince Jones		
Taylor	Bryan William	Ince Jones		1936
Thom	Alan Cameron	Dixon	1901	1916
Thomas	David H. E.	Ince Jones	1931	1939
Thomson	Arnold A. P.	Ince Jones		
Thorman	Roger	Ince Jones		
Thorpe	Raymond Banks	Ince Jones	1917	1925?
Todrick	Thomas	Dixon		
Todrick	William	Dixon		

Appendix 2

The Arnold Way

LIST OF EX-PUPILS OF THE NORTHAMPTON HIGH SCHOOL FOR THE DEAF (Cont'd)

Surname	Names	Head	Enter Year	Left Year
Valentin	Theodore	Dixon		
Vanderblank	John	Ince Jones		1933
Venville	Barry	Ince Jones	1944	
Vigne	Stephen	Ince Jones	1930	1933
Voss	Bobby	Ince Jones	1931	1939
Wallace	Seville	Ince Jones		1934
Wallbridge	Henry J.	Ince Jones		1930
Walters	Ince J.	Dixon		
Walton	G.	Ince Jones		
Watney	Vivian Eustace	Arnold		
Webb	R. A. C.	Ince Jones	1937	1940
Whitty	Norman	Ince Jones	1937	1940
Willett	Thomas	Arnold	1881	1884
Wilson	Rodney	Ince Jones	1943	1944
Wilson	David	Ince Jones	1937	1940
Wilson	Allan M.	Ince Jones	1937	1940
Wingrove	John	Ince Jones	1938	1944
Wood	B.	Ince Jones		
Wright	David John M.	Ince Jones	1934	1939
Yorke	Vivian J.	Ince Jones	1909?	
Young	Dick	Ince Jones		

Although the compilation of the list of children who were taught at Northampton High School for the Deaf from 1868 to 1945 (including Frederick A. Holt, 1860-1862) has been done as far as is possible, apologies are extended to those ex-pupils of the School whose names are not on the list.

Total number of pupils (at least) = 158

The Arnold Way

Appendix 3

Northampton High School for the Deaf

School Roll of Honour

The Honours Board was designed and painted in water-colours by Kenneth H. Pritchard, framed in oak and hung over the fireplace in the schoolroom in 1932. Mr. Ince-Jones compiled the list of boys who passed the public examinations.

1876	A. Farrar	Cambridge Local Examination
1880	A. Farrar	South Kensington Science and Art in Chemistry/ Geology.
1881	A. Farrar	London Matriculation Exam.
1887	A. Farrar	Elected F.G.S.
1892	H. Francis	3rd Class College of Preceptors.
1898	C. G. Douglas-Irvine	3rd Class College of Preceptors.
1903	Lynton Mallett	Entered St. John's College, Oxford
1904	C. G. Douglas-Irvine	Entered Edinburgh University
1907	Lynton Mallett	B.A. Degree, Oxford University
1907	N. Brunning-Maddison	Entered Royal College of Science
1907 – 11.	N. Brunning-Maddison	Exams in Chemistry, Physics, Mechanics, Geology, Astronomy, etc.
1914	E. Hodgson	Oxford Junior Local Examination.
1916	A. Banks	Oxford Junior Local.
1921	A. Bilibin	Oxford Junior Local.
1921	F. C. Smallman	Oxford Junior Local.
1922	E. J. H. Hodges	Oxford Junior Local
1923	E. J. H. Hodges	Oxford Junior Local with Hons/Distinctions.
1923	J. O. Cayley	Oxford Junior Local
1923	J. H. Gibbons	Oxford Junior Local
1925	J. O. Cayley	Oxford School Certificate
1925	E. J. H. Hodges	Oxford School Certificate
1925	P. Fischer	Oxford Junior Local with Hons.
1925	T. McClure	Oxford Junior Local
1925	F. Peacocke	Oxford Junior Local
1925	H. Shwer	Oxford Junior Local
1926	S. G. Powell	Oxford Junior Local
1927	P. Fischer	Oxford School Certificate
1928	S. G. Powell	Oxford School Certificate
1928	D. Denison	Oxford Junior Local
1928	J. Murphy	Oxford Junior Local
1928	R. A. Murphy	Oxford Junior Local
1928	B. L. Pitcher	Oxford Junior Local
1928	L. H. Pritchard	Oxford Junior Local
1928	K. H. Pritchard	Oxford Junior Local
1929	P. E. Gibbons	Oxford Junior Local
1929	F. J. Davey	Oxford Junior Local
1929	P. Fischer	Entered Cape Town University
1930	B. L. Pitcher	Oxford School Certificate
1930	H. Wallbridge	Oxford Junior Local
1931	S. Wallace	Oxford Junior Local
1931	J. Radford	Oxford Junior Local
1932	B. L. Pitcher	Entered Imperial College of Science, University of London
1932	S. G. Powell	Passed Finals as an Accountant
1932	P. H. Shillington (Fischer)	Dip. Arch., Cape Town University
1933	S. Wallace	Oxford School Certificate
1933	A.K.C. Fisher	Oxford Junior Local
1933	N. Coughlan	Oxford Junior Local
1933	J. H. Harrison	Oxford Junior Local
1933	P. J. Lewis	Oxford Junior Local
1933	B. W. Taylor	Oxford Junior Local
1934	P. H. Shillington	A.R.I.B.A., Cape Town University

1935	D. J. M. Wright	Oxford Junior Local with Distinctions
1936	A. K.C. Fisher	Oxford School Certificate
1937	B. L. Pitcher	B.Sc. Degree, Imperial College of Science, A.R.C.S. Diploma
1937	D. J. M. Wright	Oxford School Certificate
1937	R. Voss	Oxford Junior Local
1937	G. Street	Oxford Junior Local
1939	B. L. Pitcher	Ph.D., Imperial College of Science
1939	R. B. Thorpe	A.R.I.B.A.
1939	D. J. M. Wright	Entered Oriel College, University of Oxford
1942	D. J. M. Wright	B.A. Degree in English, Oriel College
1942	P. King	Oxford School Certificate
1942	M. Strong	Oxford School Certificate
1942	J. K. Wingrove	Oxford School Certificate
1943	D. Forbes	Oxford Junior Local
1943	J. Hadfield	Oxford Junior Local
1943	D. Hyslop	Oxford Junior Local
1943	M. Messer	Oxford Junior Local
1943	M. Sutton	Oxford Junior Local

Very few of the deaf boys sat for the subject of French Language. It had to be taken in the Oxford School Certificate because a foreign language was compulsory. It was the reason why, though so many boys passed the Oxford Junior examinations, only a few of them passed the School Certificate.

ENGLISH ESSAY.

Thursday, December 12th, 1918. 1¼ Hours.

Write an Essay on **one** of the following subjects:

(1) Holiday work on the land.

(2) "A rolling stone gathers no moss."

(3) "The grand old name of gentleman
Defamed by every charlatan
And soiled with all ignoble use."

(4) Children in the plays of Shakespeare **or** in any novels you have read.

PRÉCIS WRITING.

Thursday, December 12th, 1918. 1¼ Hours.

Candidates are desired to give *in their own words* the substance of the following passage. The Précis should present in a consecutive and readable shape, briefly and distinctly expressed, the main points of the passage, so that any one who has not time to read the passage itself may learn the substance of it from the Précis.

[*It is suggested that from 300 to 500 words will probably be a reasonable length for this Précis. Candidates can sufficiently ascertain whether their versions fall within these limits, by multi-*

An example from the Oxford School Certificate: English Essay, 1918
Courtesy of British Library. (Ref. 8366.K.13)

The Arnold Way

Appendix 4

The Prospectus of the Northampton High School for the Deaf issued in the 1910s

History of School

THIS SCHOOL was founded in 1868 by Dr. T. Arnold, one of the highest authorities on the education of the deaf. He was succeeded by Mr. H. N. Dixon, M.A., F.L.S., who retired in 1909. Mr. Ince Jones, B.Sc., the present Principal, was associated with Mr. Dixon from 1901.

It is the only School of its kind in this country which has been under the control of University men.

Special Aim

Its special aim is to give deaf boys as varied and advanced an education as hearing boys. That this aim has been realised is shown by the fact that boys while pupils at the School, though stone deaf from birth or early infancy, have passed the following remarkable list of public examinations.

LONDON MATRICULATION.
CAMBRIDGE JUNIOR LOCAL.
COLLEGE OF PRECEPTORS.
SOUTH KENSINGTON IN CHEMISTRY (Theoretical and Practical).
SOUTH KENSINGTON IN ART.

Success of Pupils

Old boys have gone on to Oxford, Edinburgh, and London Universities, and one of Mr. Ince Jones' old pupils, after a successful course as an ordinary student at the Royal College of Science, has taken up the career of analytical chemist.

The method of instruction employed is that known as the Oral System, under which Speech and Lip-reading are the means of communication.

As it is very important that the education of the deaf should start early, boys can be admitted at any time after the age of four.

This school is suitable for any boys who are too deaf to benefit by an ordinary school.

Special care is taken to maintain, and if possible to develop residual hearing.

Lip-reading lessons are given to those who have lost their hearing in later life.

Stammering and other defects of speech are treated.

The School is very healthily situated in its own grounds. It stands high, facing the open country and overlooking the Valley of the Nene.

Northampton is centrally situated, 1¼ hours from Euston on the L. and N.W. Railway main line, and is also on the Midlands Railway.

If necessary, boys can be met at London, Rugby, etc.

AIMS OF THE SCHOOL

The special aim of the School is to give deaf boys an education as varied and advanced as is open to their hearing brothers. That this aim has been realised is shown by the success of its pupils in Public Examinations. Boys attending the School, though stone deaf from birth or early infancy, have passed the following Examinations:—

Matriculation (London University)
*Oxford Senior Local
*Oxford Junior Local
Cambridge Junior Local
College of Preceptors
South Kensington in Art, Chemistry (Theoretical and Practical), etc.

Domestic Arrangements

These are in the hands of the Matron, a fully-qualified trained teacher of the deaf with long experience of deaf and hearing children of all ages. Parents may have every confidence in leaving very young children in her care. The School is as much as possible like home.

Boys should bring :—
- Cricket and Football Clothes.
- 2 pairs of Sheets.
- Pillow Cases.
- 3 Bath Towels and 3 Chamber Towels.
- 3 Napkins and Ring.
- Fish Knife and Fork.
- A Rug and a Mackintosh.

School Colours are dark green,

Terms

100 guineas a year, payable in advance each term. A term's notice is required before removal of a pupil.

Special terms can sometimes be arranged for very young boys.

Principal . . F. INCE-JONES, B.Sc. (Lond.)
Lecturer and Examiner to the National College of Teachers of the Deaf
Barrister-at-Law of the Inner Temple
Assisted by a Fully Qualified and University Staff

Telephone: Northampton 1581

Appendix 4

The Arnold Way

Games, etc. All boys, unless exempted on medical grounds, are required to join in the out-door games. Association football in the winter and spring terms, and cricket in the summer term are played with hearing boys of normal schools.

Lawn tennis is played in the school grounds.

An Athletic Sports Day is held in conjunction with a normal school.

Regular Swedish and Military Drill are taught.

In the summer boys go regularly to the swimming baths, which are very near the school.

Workshops There are excellent workshops, where the boys learn Woodwork of all kinds under an experienced teacher.

There is also a Museum and Chemical Laboratory.

Boys are taught Gardening in its various branches.

Arrangements can be made for Golf, Painting and Dancing.

Holidays There are three holidays during the year; about four weeks at Christmas, three weeks at Easter, and seven weeks in the summer.

Below is taken from the 1930s prospectus of the School

REFERENCES (Parents or Relatives of Pupils).

PRINCE and PRINCESSE BAGRATION, La Feuille, Champel, Geneva.
LADY BALL, 9 Pembroke Park, Clyde Road, Dublin.
The LADY BATTERSEA, The Pleasaunce, Overstrand, Norfolk.
H. ATTWOOD, Esq., and Mrs ATTWOOD, Woodlands, Hartlebury, Kidderminster.
W. S. CALDER, Esq., and Mrs. CALDER, Ravensthorpe, Harborne, Birmingham.
Mrs. CAYLEY, Hopecroft, Barton-on-Sea, Hants.
Miss CHAPPELL, Dipley, Winchfield, Hants.
Colonel CHEREMETEFF, Paris.
The Rev. Canon H. HAM and Mrs. HAM, Cathedral Vicarage, Derby.
Mrs. HARVEY GOODWIN, 9 Portland Square, Carlisle.
General SIR DAVID KINLOCH, Bart., C.B., M.V.O., Gilmerton, Drem., N.B.
Mrs. KINLOCH, Gilmerton Ranch, Cliffside, Shawinigan Lake, Vancouver Is.
The Ven. ARCHDEACON of KILDARE and Mrs. PEACOCKE, Kill Rectory, Co. Kildare.
Capt. OSWALD MARSHALL, C.B.E., and Mrs. MARSHALL, 13 Emperors Gate, S.W.
ALEX. McCLURE, Esq., and Mrs. McCLURE, 132 West Regent St., Glasgow, and 2 Bellhauston Terrace, Ibrox, Glasgow.
Capt. L. H. PRITCHARD and Mrs. PRITCHARD, The Glade, Green Lane, Stanmore.
ALLAN THOM, Esq., and Mrs. THOM, Island of Canna, Inverness-shire.
A. J. YORKE, Esq., Gwernant, Kingstonridge, Lewes.

Reference is also kindly permitted to:

The Most Hon. the MARQUESS of EXETER, C.M.G., Burleigh House, Stamford.
The Rt. Hon. LORD CHARNWOOD (President of the National Association of Teachers of the Deaf), Stowe House, Lichfield.
The Rt. Hon. LORD HENLEY, Watford Court, Rugby.
The Rt. Hon. LORD EBBISHAM, 17 Abchurch Lane, London, E.C.4.
The Rt. Revd. The LORD BISHOP OF PETERBOROUGH, The Palace, Peterborough.
The Rt. Revd. BISHOP TALBOT (Late Bishop of Winchester) and The Hon. Mrs. TALBOT, Lexham Gardens, London.
SIR JOSIAH STAMP, G.B.E., D.Sc., Tantallon, Shortlands, Kent.
The Hon. and Revd. CANON E. LYTTELTON, D.D. (Late Headmaster of Eton).
E. BROUGHTON BARNES Esq., F.R.C.S., Nine Springs, Northampton.
Colonel JOHN BROWN, C.B., D.S.O., Harpole, Northampton.
BERNARD CAMPION, Esq., K.C., 3 Grays Inn Square, London.
E. HARRIES-JONES, Esq., M.D., 16 Castilian Street, Northampton.
J. KERR LOVE, Esq., M.D., F.R.C.S., Glasgow.
The Revd. CANON F. S. KEYSELL, Benefield Rectory, Oundle, Northampton.
The Revd. G. C. LUNT and Mrs. LUNT, The Vicarage, Portsea, Hants.
G. HAY MORGAN, Esq., K.C., 15 Hamilton Terrace, St. Johns Wood, London.
A. J. STORY, Esq. (Sec. National Institute for the Deaf,) 2 Bloomsbury St., W.
MACLEOD YEARDSLEY, Esq., F.R.C.S., 81 Wimpole St., Cavendish Sq., London, W.

The Arnold Way ## Appendix 5(a)

Spring Hill School Groups

Spring Hill School, 1925
Back: Row: L. Pritchard, E. Hodges, P. Fischer
Next Row: O. Cayley, R. Sawdon, J. Murphy, E. Gourley, Tom McClure, _____, Dick Young
Seated: Mr. Mundin, F. Smallman, _____, Mrs. Ince-Jones, Mr. Ince-Jones, _____, Miss Knowles
Front Row: J. Attwood, _____, W. Coates, R. Murphy, K. Pritchard, _____

Courtesy of Derek Pritchard

Appendix 5(a)

The Arnold Way

Spring Hill School Groups

Staff and boys in 1927

Back Row: B. Pitcher, G. Proctor, P. Gibbons. J. Murphy, J. Attwood, L. Pritchard, R. Murphy, K. Pritchard, J. Hill, D. Denison

Middle Row: Mr. Baxter, Miss Sandiford, S. Powell, R. Thorpe, Mrs. Ince-Jones with Patricia, Mr. Ince-Jones, Miss Lawrence, P. Fischer, (French Mistress), Mr. E. Mundin

Front Row: B. Taylor, N. Maltass, J. Cobley, A. Fisher, G. Paton, C. Ham, H. Cope, J. England, F. Davey

Courtesy of Philip Gibbons

Appendix 5(a)

Spring Hill School, 1930

Top Row: S. Wallace, H. Wallbridge, K. Pritchard, J. Hill, L. Pritchard, P. Gibbons, R. Murphy, P. Lewis, B. Pitcher, F. Davey
Middle Row: J. Dalton, J. Radford, N. Glenn, _____ (Teacher), Mr. Mundin, Mrs. Ince-Jones, Mr. Ince-Jones, Miss Cox (Matron), Mr. Baxter, Miss Milton, C. Ham, T. Dalmau
Bottom Row: J. Cobley, N. Coughlan, N. Maltass, G. Paton, Patricia Ince-Jones, _____, G. Radford, B. Taylor, A. Fisher, J. England

Courtesy of Philip Gibbons

Appendix 5(a)

The Arnold Way

Spring Hill School, 1938

Top Row: B. Voss, C. Ham, G. Salomon, T. Adams, E. Cox, D. Thomas, J. Wright, P. Lewis, G. Street, N. Whitty, G. Fair, P. Melvin
Middle Row: W. Jenkins, J. Napier, Miss Cox, Miss Richardson, Mrs. Mundin, Mr. Mundin, Mr. Ince-Jones, Mrs. Ince-Jones, Mr. Baxter, Miss Milton, T. Webb, G. Knowles
Bottom Row: D. Hyslop, A. Wilson, W. Adams, J. Pickworth, D. Wilson, D. Forbes, M. Messer, A. Cuthbertson

Courtesy of David Hyslop

The Arnold Way   **Appendix 5(a)**

Spring Hill School, 1941

Top Row: M. Sutton, D. Hyslop, J. Wingrove, M. Strong, M. Gent, P. Melvin, D. Forbes, P. Hood, P. King.
Middle Row: Pamela Ince-Jones, J. Pickworth, Miss Richardson, Mrs. Mundin, Mr. Mundin, Mr. Ince-Jones, Mrs. Ince-Jones, Mr. Baxter, Miss R. Milton, W. Adams, D. Evans, Patricia Ince-Jones
Bottom Row: W. Clay, S. Barkes, J. Scott, R. Drewry, J. Hadfield, G. Drewry.

Appendix 5(b) *The Arnold Way*

Spring Hill School Cricket Teams

Back Row: P. Melvin, P. Lewis, D. Thomas, J. Wright, G. Street (scorer), T. Adams, T. Webb,
Front Row: G. Knowles, W. Jenkins, Mr Mundin, Mr. Ince-Jones, C. Ham, R. Voss
Spring Hill Magazine, 1938

Back Row: M. Gent, P. Wingrove, M. Sutton, P. Hood, D. Forbes, J. Hadfield (scorer)
Front Row: D. Hyslop, M. Strong, Mr. Mundin, Mr. Ince-Jones, P. Melvin, P. King
Spring Hill Magazine, 1941

The Arnold Way ## Appendix 5(b)

Spring Hill School Cricket Team

Back Row: M. Messer (scorer), M. Gent, K. Perry, J. Wingrove, D. Forbes, M. Sutton, K. Stephens
Front Row:, P. King, M. Strong, Mr. Ince-Jones. Mr. Mundin, D. Hyslop

Back Row: J. Hadfield (scorer), K. Stephens, M. Sutton, M.Gent, M. Messer, K. Perry, B.Haycox. S. Barkes
Front Row: D. Forbes, P. King, Mr. Ince-Jones, Mr. Mundin, D. Hyslop, J. Wingrove
Spring Hill Magazine, 1943

Appendix 5(c)

The Arnold Way

Spring Hill School Football Teams

Back Row: G. Knowles, P. Melvin, D. Thomas, T. Adams, N. Glenn. G. Paton
Front Row: W. Jenkins, P. Lewis, C. Ham, N. Coughlan, R. Voss
Photo by C. D. Ham, Spring Hill Magazine, 1937

Back Row: R. Webb, P. Melvin, D. Thomas, J. Wright, N.. Whitty, G. Knowles,
Front Row: D. Hyslop, M. Messer, P. Lewis, C. Ham, R. Voss, A. Cuthbertson, D. Wilson
Spring Hill Magazine, 1939

The Arnold Way   **Appendix 5(c)**

Spring Hill School Football Teams

Back Row: S. Barkes, B. Haycox, D. Forbes, J. Wingrove, M. Sutton, J. Hadfield
Front Row: M. Gent, D. Hyslop, M. Strong, P. King, P. Hood
Spring Hill Magazine, 1942

Back Row: G. Drewry, J. Hadfield, R. Monins, J. Pickworth, B. Haycox, D. Myers, S. Barkes
Front Row: M. Sutton, D. Forbes, D. Hyslop, R. Wilson, K. Stephens
Spring Hill Magazine, 1944

Appendix 5(d) *The Arnold Way*

The Pritchard Photographic Collection (1)
(1917—1932)

A group of boys at Spring Hill, 1919

Tennis Party

Spring Hill Cricketers

The Arnold Way   **Appendix 5(d)**

The Pritchard Photographic Collection (2)
(1917—1932)

Appendix 5(d)

The Arnold Way

The Pritchard Photographic Collection (3)
(1917—1932)

Left to right: ***Lyonel Pritchard, Pat Fischer, Kenneth Pritchard***

Appendix 5(d)

The Pritchard Photographic Collection (4)
(1917—1932)

Appendix 5(e) *The Arnold Way*

Philip E. Gibbons Photographic Collection

Philip Gibbons, Jack Attwood, Bryan Taylor

Swimming Cups

B. Pitcher, K. Pritchard, R. Murphy

The Arnold Way **Appendix 5(e)**

Philip E. Gibbons Photographic Collection (2)

Tennis in action. Note a boy sitting on the ladder, umpiring the game.

***View of Spring Hill
House at South East End***

***View of Spring Hill
House at North East End***

Appendix 5(e)

The Arnold Way

Philip E. Gibbons Photographic Collection (3)

The Tennis Party at Spring Hill, 1928
Back Row: K. Pritchard, J. Hill, . L. Pritchard, D. Denison
Kneeling: Jack Attwood, R. Murphy, S. Powell, B. Pitcher, P. Gibbons, Jack Murphy
Seated on Ground: J. Cobley, A. Fisher, _____, Brian Taylor, C. Ham, _____, N. Maltass, _____, J. England

Freddy Davey, P. Gibbons

The Arnold Way

Appendix 5(e)

Philip E. Gibbons Photographic Collection (4)
(1917—-1932)

Back Row: P. Gibbons, J. Hill, J. Dalton, K. Pritchard, R. Murphy, B. Pitcher, D. Denison
Middle Row: F. Davey, S. Wallace, J. England, J. Napier, B. Taylor, C. Ham (behind), _____
Front Row: _____, G. Paton

Back Row: C. Ham, K. Pritchard, R. Murphy, D. Denison (behind), B. Pitcher, S. Wallace, J. Hill, F. Davey
Middle Row: _____, N. Maltass, J. Cobley, J. Wright, J. Attwood, H. Wallbridge, J. Dalton, P. Gibbons
Next Row: Brian Taylor, G. Radford, J. Radford, A. Fisher
Front Row:, _____, G. Paton,

Appendix 6 — *The Arnold Way*

Notes.

1. Abbreviations.

YIDD	Yorkshire Institution for the Deaf and Dumb
NATD	National Association of Teachers of the Deaf
NCTD	National College of Teachers of the Deaf
BDDA	British Deaf and Dumb Association
CTDD	College of Teachers of the Deaf and Dumb
MHGS	Mary Hare Grammar School for the Deaf

2. Ex-pupils of Miss Mary Hare's Oral School for the Deaf, Dene Hollow, Burgess Hill.

The following pupils of Spring Hill were transferred from Mary Hare's Oral School for the Deaf, Dene Hollow, Burgess Hill, (total = 17 pupils):

- ADAMS, Terry
- HOOD, Paul
- LEWIS, Philip
- MESSER, Michael
- MORRIS, Allan
- NAPIER, John
- SMALLMAN, Frederick
- SUTTON, Michael
- WHITTY, Norman
- GOODE, Brian
- KNOWLES, Geoffrey
- MARSHALL, Michael
- MONINS, Ray
- MURRAY, Richard
- PITCHER, Bernard
- STEPHENS, Keith
- WILSON, Rodney

Source of reference: Boyce, A.J. & Lavery, E., *The Lady in Green*, BDHS pub. 1999

3. Biographies.

The following biographical sketches of ex-pupils of the Northampton High School for the Deaf can be found in Jackson, P.W. & Lee, Raymond, *Deaf Lives,* BDHS pub. 2001.

- Cyril Carr
- Abraham Farrar
- Bernard Lewis Pitcher
- David John Murray Wright

4. Northampton Deaf History.

The earliest reference to the deaf and to deafness at Northampton relates to Daniel Whalley, the son of Peter Whalley who twice held the office of mayoralty of Northampton in 1646-7 and 1655-6.

It was in 1660 that Dr. John Wallis, a well-known professor of Mathematics at the University of Oxford, was informed about Daniel Whalley by his friends who read Dr. Wallis's treatise on Speech, which mentioned that it was possible to teach a deaf person to speak. He agreed to make a trial of it on Daniel, who came to Oxford in January 1661. This young *deaf and dumb* man became deaf at the age of five. After a year Daniel could pronounce distinctly any word. He was also taught to understand the English language and to express himself in writing. He read most of the Bible and understood the historical part of it. He could read and understand letters addressed to him and to reply to them. It is recorded that on May 21 1662 Dr. Wallis took the 25 years-old Daniel and another deaf pupil, Alexander Popham to the Royal Society and demonstrated on how the deaf could be taught. Later he did the same before King Charles II and his courtiers. At that time, the idea of the deaf being capable of education was unheard of and so it was quite an achievement for Dr. Wallis. Daniel Whalley died at Cogenhoe in 1695. (See *Deaf Lives* published by the British Deaf History Society, 2001, and A. Farrar's *An Unpublished Account of Dr. Wallis and his Deaf Pupils* in *The Teacher of the Deaf,* February 1927.)

The most notable and interesting Deaf character in the vicinity of Northampton was Ambrose Isted (1797 – 1881) of Ecton Hall. He was famous for his hunting activities with the Pytchley Hunt and for his sketches of the local hunting scenes. He attended the London Asylum for the Deaf and Dumb as a private pupil of the celebrated headmaster, Dr. Joseph Watson. He could communicate using signs and fingerspelling and used pencil and paper when communicating with hearing people at large. An extract from a poem written by Matthew Fortescue around 1828 on the Pytchley Hunt reads:-

Then Isted prepar'd for the chase has no doubt,
To get his first place when he's mounted on Gout;
But he had been wrong to have back'd his good luck,
As Gout and his rider fell slap in a brook;

Courtesy of Local History Studies, Central Public Library, Northampton

This was Ambrose and his chestnut horse, Gout. Ambrose earned the nickname *The Deaf Squire of Ecton* and was very well respected in the village of Ecton and known for his charitable deeds. He is unique as the only Deaf Master of the traditional English hunting as to date. Full details can be found in *Deaf History Journal,* August 1998, and *Deaf Lives.*

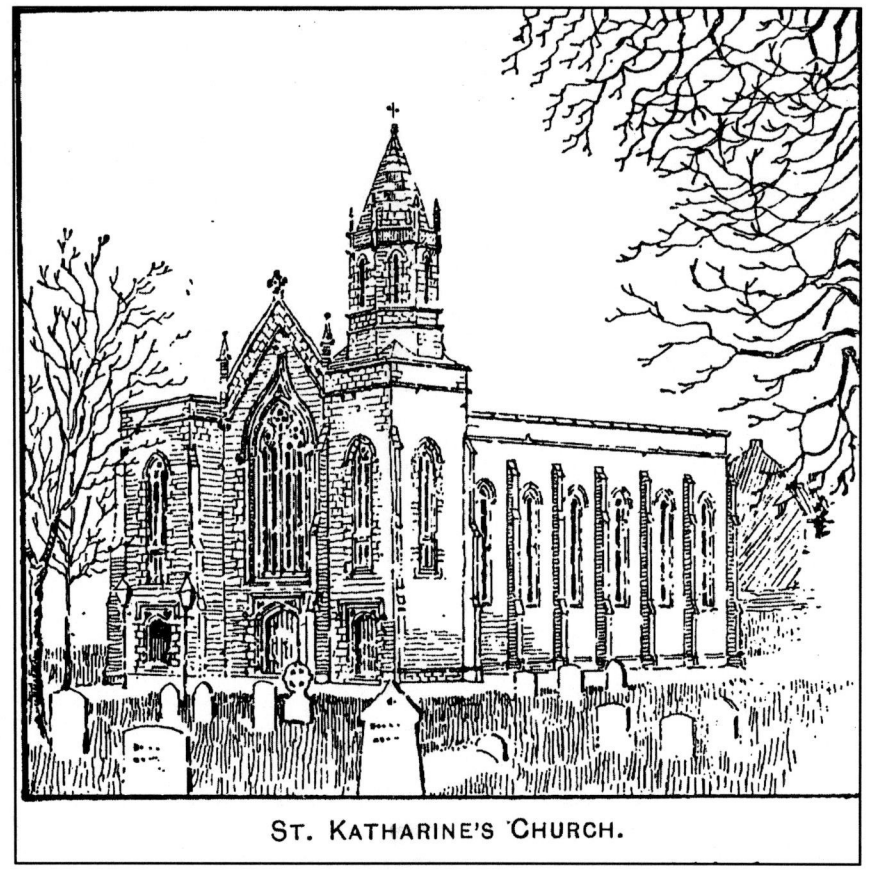

Ephphatha Magazine for the Deaf,
Courtesy of RNID Library

Appendix 6
The Arnold Way

It will be recalled that in Chapter 1, when Thomas Arnold was at the YIDD, Doncaster, during the early 1840s, William Sleight was one of his teaching colleagues. Sleight left Doncaster to become the headmaster of the Brighton Institution for the Deaf and Dumb in Sussex. One of his sons was the Reverend William Blomfield Sleight (1849 – 1929) and, after obtaining his degree at Clare College, Cambridge University, he moved to Northampton to become the curate of St. Katharine's Church in 1874 and became a priest in 1877. In 1880 he left for Swadlincote, Derbyshire, but returned to Northampton 9 years later as the Vicar of St. Katharine's Church. He started the first church services for the Deaf on Sunday afternoons at his Northampton church and used the combined system of communication with the Deaf community.

From 1890 to 1913, the Rev. W. B. Sleight held the Presidency of the British Deaf and Dumb Association and was one of the Royal Commissioners of 1886 - 89 appointed to enquire into the educational problems of deafness and blindness. He was for many years one of the Board members of the Northampton High School for Girls. It was due to him that an institute for deaf adults was set up in Northampton in connection with the Peterborough and Leicester Diocesan Adult Deaf Christian Welfare Society. The institute was at Seymour Place near St. Katharine's Church.

The Northampton and County Mission to the Deaf and Dumb was then formed as a branch of the Leicester County Mission and church services were held at the Seymour Place with the help of Leslie Edwards the Leicester Deaf missioner. During the annual general meeting of 1923 held at St. Giles' Church Buildings, one of the speakers was a Miss Risbee who spoke about the establishment of the school in Northampton by the Rev. Thomas Arnold and carried on first by Mr. H. N. Dixon and *now by Mr. Ince- Jones*. Her speech was *translated by the fingers of Miss Richards* for the benefit of the Deaf audience.

The Rev. W. B. Sleight

The Deaf Institute, Seymour Place, Northampton

In 1928 Mr. Algernon J. M. Barnett (1884 – 1953), born deaf, was appointed the first full-time Missioner in the Diocese of Northants and Rutland and proved to be popular with the local community because of his cheerful outlook. In July 1930 the old St. Peter's Schools in

Green Street were purchased for conversion into the new institute and chapel. In November 1931 the Seymour Place institute was closed and the Green Street premises were opened on November 10 1931. Mr. Barnett, or Algy as he was called, continued his missionary work with the deaf until his death in early 1953.

His ever-ready smile brought a comment from a police constable on patrol one dismal Sunday morning, "Good morning Mr. Barnett, you have brought the sunshine". He was a household name throughout the diocese of Northants and Rutland, visiting every town and village [by bus and walk], *making collections from door to door to keep the mission in funds.*

In 1929 Mr. Barnett visited a local school for hearing boys in Kettering and found Gunn, a deaf boy, who experienced some difficulties at school. *After many setbacks and delays caused by the education officers, and especially by the boy's father, who at first strongly opposed the idea of his son being sent to the School for the Deaf, but in the end waived his objection* and Mr. Barnett succeeded in getting the deaf lad into the School for the Deaf – *at Birmingham.*

Photo: Mr. Lawrie (Caretaker of the Deaf Institute), Saville Wallace, Philip Gibbons, Algernon Barnett, Kenneth Pritchard outside St. Mark's Church, Northampton.. Undated.
Courtesy of Derek Pritchard

It is interesting to note that Mr. Philip Gibbons was the only pupil from Spring Hill School to visit the Deaf Club whilst at school and after meeting Mr. Barnett, they became great friends. He commented that Mr. Ince-Jones never talked about the Deaf Club. A photo was taken in 1933 when they posed outside St. Mark's Church. Further details on Mr. Algernon Barnett can be found in *Deaf Lives*.

So much for the brief history of the Northampton Deaf Community.

5. Frederick Samuel Ellis Holt (1846 – 1902)

Frederick Holt was born in 1846 and deafened from scarlet fever at the age of eight years. After his stay in England with the Rev. Thomas Arnold at Northampton and with his uncle at Harrogate, he returned to Australia in 1875. He married and had four children. He was killed in a railway accident at the age of 56. His family still live in Sydney. His eldest son was for some years a director of the New South Wales Institution for the Deaf and Dumb, Australia, founded in 1860.

Information from Thomas S. Holt to Jean Walter, *The Teacher of the Deaf*, February 1958.

6. Rollo Havee Dixon (1862 -   )

Rollo Dixon was born *deaf and dumb* in 1862 at Witham/Wickham Bishops, Essex. His father was a farmer of 130 acres and employed six men to do the farming business. At first Rollo Dixon was a private pupil of Gerrit van Asche, who used the oral method of communication at Burlington Street, Chorlton as revealed in the 1871 Manchester census. In 1874 he moved to Northampton to continue his oral education, this time, under the Rev. Thomas Arnold. After a few years, he left to join his father at Witham and took an apprenticeship in gardening. He was said to be married with some children, living in Hampshire.

7. Mr. H.N. Dixon's views on Rev. Thomas Arnold.

Mr. Dixon's article on the late Thomas Arnold taken from the *Northamptonshire Notes and Queries* reads:-

Mr. Arnold's writings are distinctly of the analytical and deductive order; his vein was a philosophical one, and he always chose to search out the underlying principles of things and thence to deduce the true method of their practical application, rather than to generalise from observed facts. Indeed one is rather struck by the comparative absence from his writings of conclusions based on his own experience as a teacher. Even when he deals with the practical details of teaching, his rules and suggestions are usually founded on as application of principles he has previously evolved on general considerations. This gives a logical sequence and a general roundedness and completeness to his system of teaching which is its main characteristic, and which does not lose its value from the fact that in practice deviations from the rules laid down are often necessary. So, too, in his strenuous advocacy of the oral system, while manualists may reasonably claim that in certain cases and under adverse conditions the teaching of speech and language by means of speech may be impracticable or inadvisable, few we think will deny that Mr. Arnold has shown by a logical argument based on sound and philosophical considerations, that speech is the natural medium of communication for the deaf as well as for the hearing; that is cultivating this faculty we are helping Nature to follow out her own course, and in so doing we may therefore expect to receive from her the readiest response. To have placed a system of education which was, as he found it, almost entirely on a empirical one, on a sound and philosophical basis, and to have demonstrated by his own teaching its practical value, is no unworthy result of a life's work; this among many other labours, it may fairly be claimed that Mr. Arnold has done for the oral system: and it is by this that, as he himself would most desire, his name will be longest remembered.

(Thomas Arnold died on January 21 1897 and was buried at the Northampton Cemetery. The polished red Aberdeen granite memorial with its square plinth and pedestal with ornamental copings stood eight feet high over the grave of Thomas Arnold. There is also another memorial, a white marble tablet placed in Doddridge Church.)

8. Views of Mr. F. Ince-Jones on the Rev. Thomas Arnold.

Mr. F. Ince-Jones was the President of the National College of Teachers of the Deaf in

Appendix 6

March 1932, Chairman of the NCTD Examinations Board from 1929 to 1944 and the Examiner on the History of Education of the Deaf. He wrote in *The Teacher of the Deaf*, August 1941:-

In the course of long years during which, as examiner in the History of the Education of the Deaf, I have marked a large number of papers. I have found certain mistakes and misapprehensions crop up regularly with regard to that great teacher, Thomas Arnold.

One is that he was a blacksmith. I do not know how this has arisen. For a short time he assisted his father at cabinet-making, but he was never a smith. Another is that he was a clergyman who held several livings. As a matter of fact he was a Congregationalist minister and for twenty years in Northampton was the Minister of Doddridge Church, famous for the ministry of Philip Doddridge, author of such well-known hymns as "O God of Bethel," and "Hark the glad sound the saviour comes." For twenty years he contrived to carry out both his ministerial and his school duties, but ultimately he gave up his important ministry in one of the largest churches in the town in order to devote himself fully to his teaching of the deaf.

The most curious error, however, is that Arnold had not much experience of teaching but is notable for his writings. It is true his books are a permanent monument to his fame; one of them at least is still in use nearly fifty years after his death and they constitute by far the greatest contribution ever made to the literature of the education of the deaf until then. It is true also that his writings were based upon broad fundamental educational and philosophical principles, but they were enriched and made practical by his ripe and comprehensive experience as a teacher over long years.

Arnold was never headmaster of a big institution; he had not that experience, though he had taught in such a school. But he had more than thirty years experience of teaching ranging from the most elementary to the most advanced. The headmaster of a large school or institution today enjoys much less time for actual teaching; much of his time must be spent in administration. In this sense Arnold had greater teaching experience than most, though the bulk of it was in a comparatively small school. In point of fact no teacher of the deaf can teach anything like so many pupils as a teacher in a normal school and very often confines himself to one particular type of more or less advanced child. Arnold on the other hand taught all grades of the deaf, both boys and girls and many of these from the outset to the close of their school life.

Moreover he may be regarded as the pioneer of higher education for the deaf in this country.

In 1881, Mr. Farrar, to whom the deaf and their teachers owe so much, not only for his re-writing of Arnold's Manual, but for many other acts of kindness and wisdom, including his gifts of valuable books to Manchester University, passed the London Matriculation Examination. This was a unique achievement for a deaf boy and it must be remembered that the London Matriculation of those days was definitely a harder examination to pass than it is today. Indeed many good judges think it was as difficult as a pass degree at the older universities.

The Northampton School founded by Arnold in 1868 has had an unbroken existence for seventy three years and claims to be the oldest private school for the deaf in the world. Its record is not inconsiderable. Arnold's portrait hangs in the big schoolroom. One of his desks is still in use, "Though mangled, hacked and hewn, not yet destroyed." His original language lessons – and very good they are – remain in my possession, as do his set of coloured charts, devised by Friedrich Moritz Hill.

Appendix 6

It may therefore be maintained that Arnold's spirit still lives, not only in his books, but in the continuous stream of secondary education inspired by his teaching and going on today in his own school. He being dead yet speaketh.

9. Spring Hill House and its Premises.

Mr. John Hensman was a well-known solicitor and a clerk for the Borough of Northampton for many years. In the Northampton census of 1851 there were two "cottages" sited in Spring Mounts and one of them belonged to Mr. Hensman. The word Spring Hill is first mentioned in a policy of the Phoenix Assurance Company dated in 1854 (preserved by the Local Studies Department, Northampton Central Public Library) in which is revealed that Mr. John Hensman was the owner of a dwelling house (a bricked and slated building) called Spring Hill Cottage, Northampton, insured for £1,000. Also included was the Stable and Coach-House. It was situated on the south of Billing Road and, as there were new large mansions appearing at the same time, it meant that Spring Hill House was probably built in the early 1850s. The other cottage in Spring Mounts was Springfield Cottage. The elite area covering Spring Hill, Springfield and other newly built mansions was by 1875 named Cliftonville.

John Hensman
Courtesy of Local History Studies, Northampton

It is interesting to note that short base-walls of yellow sandstone were built to form the boundaries of the west and south sides of Spring Hill premises. Iron palisades were probably stuck onto the top of these walls at first.

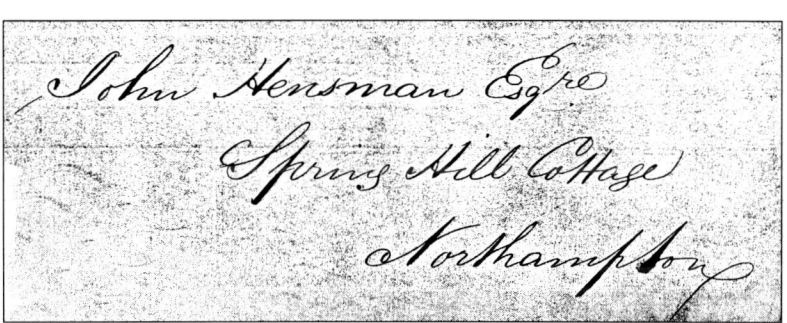

When Mr. J. Hensman died in November 1890, his wife took over the Spring Hill premises followed by a son of theirs in 1893. In 1898 Mr. John R. Buxton was found to be the owner of the premises and resided there until he vacated it in 1911, but he still owned it. As from 1912, Mr. Ince-Jones probably rented the premises and then owned the property after the death of Mr. Buxton in 1919. Maps of the Cliftonville area reveal that the two-storied extension on the eastern side of Spring Hill House was built just before the turn of the 20th century. This extension included the Dining-room and the extra first floor bedrooms. The building of the "large schoolroom" is only shown on Cliftonville maps from 1913 onwards, which meant that it was probably built in the early 1890s.

It is not known when the iron palisades were replaced by bricked walls which were built onto the top of the yellow sandstone based walls. The photograph of Cliftonville Road and the Stables (shown on page 26) taken in the early 1930s reveals, after the entrance of the Spring Hill, the presence of the high bricked boundary wall.

Appendix 6

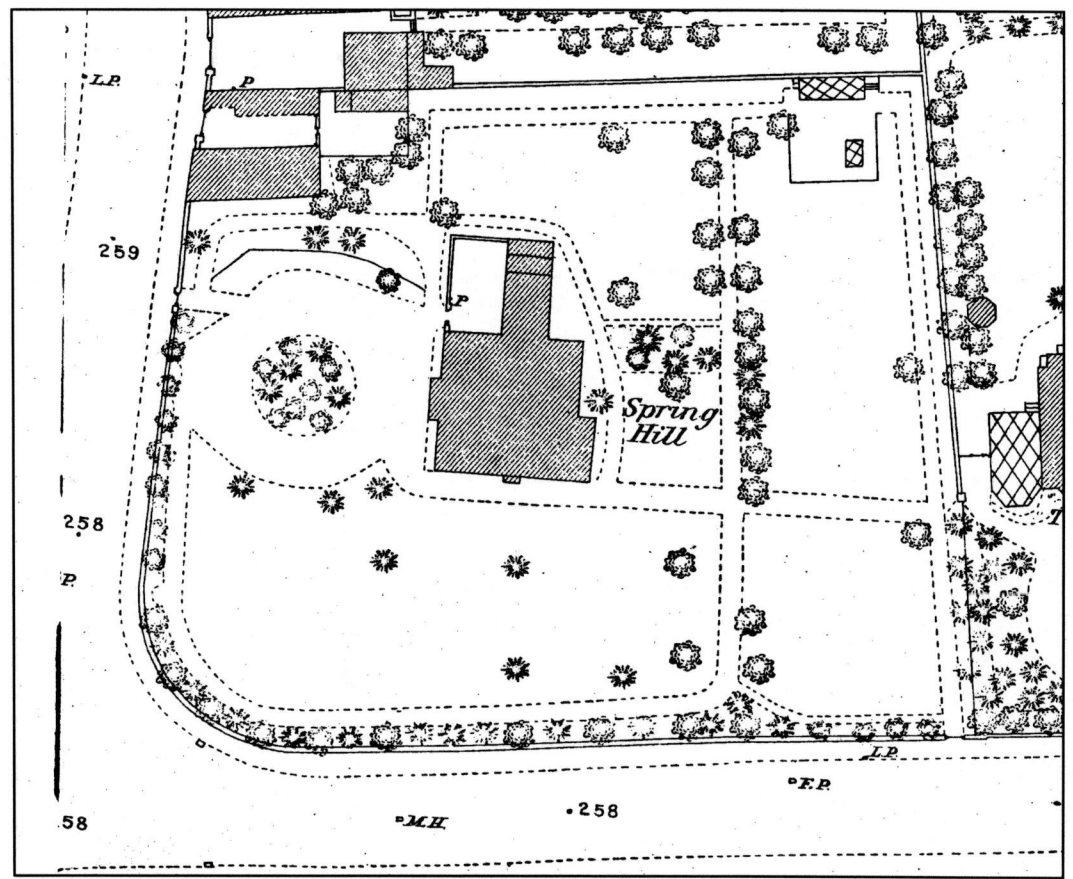

1885 Map showing Spring Hill
Note: The extended building on the east side of the House and the stable (converted to a schoolroom)
have not yet been built.
Courtesy of Local History Studies, Northampton

Springfield Cottage was erected by Mr. Latchmore, a rope merchant, who bought the land in 1846 from Northampton Borough Council. It was then sold to Mr. W. T. Portal, a wine merchant, in 1853. Then it was put up for sale in 1889 and its particulars (preserved at the Northampton Local Studies Department) could be described almost similar to those of Spring Hill thus giving an insight into its initial setting up.

Its description is as follows:-

> *All that Charming and Commodious Suburban*
> ** VILLA * RESIDENCE * known as "SPRINGFIELD,"*
> *Situate in CLIFTONVILLE, Northampton*
>
> *The House ... is pleasantly situated in beautifully secluded ornamental grounds of about one acre and commands extensive rural and urban views.*
> *On the Ground floor are Entance Hall, Study, Breakfast-room, lofty and well-proportioned Dining-room, 26ft by 19ft with large bay window; Drawing-room, Store closet, Kitchen, Servants' Hall, Servants' Summer-room, Larder, w.c.'s, ... and other Offices.*
> *In the Basement, and accessible from the dining room by a separate staircase, is a fine Billiard-room ... There are also two capital Wine Cellars and a Beer Cellar.*
> *On the first floor are five principal Bedrooms, ...*
> *There are also a two-stall Stable and loose Box, Coach-house and Harness-room, Hay and Straw Loft, Boot and Knife House, w.c., Coal and Wood Shed,...*

Appendix 6

The Arnold Way

After the closure of Spring Hill High School for the Deaf in 1945, the Northampton High School for Girls purchased the whole premises in order to establish a preparatory school for girls. Many changes were made. What was once the library staffroom became the Staff Room. Mr. Ince-Jones's daughters' own bedroom on the ground floor was converted into classrooms and enlarged along with an upstairs room. There was a coal fire in the Hall which heated three radiators. *"The schoolroom was very cold in the winters."*

One recalled :-
I remember the interior of Spring Hill with its shutters, marble fireplaces, the highly polished brass rail on the stairs, the carved fireplace in the Dining Room, the plaster swans in the archway and the downstairs ceilings with their beautiful mouldings. One glanced at the ceiling and said it's like a wedding cake.

The Headmistress of the girls' school remarked, *"Spring Hill has a lovely homely atmosphere and I don't think we should let this change."*

After the closure of this school in 1989, St. Andrew's Hospital acquired the Spring Hill premises and uses it as a residential nursing care home. Spring Hill House and the lawns remain as they were, but the sight of new high buildings and extensions, built behind at the north and north-east side of the House, is sadly an eye-sore to passers-by.

The Arnold Way   **Appendix 7**

Sketched plan of Spring Hill premises on 1 acre plot
(not drawn to scale)
Based on the sketches by George Drewry (1939—1945)

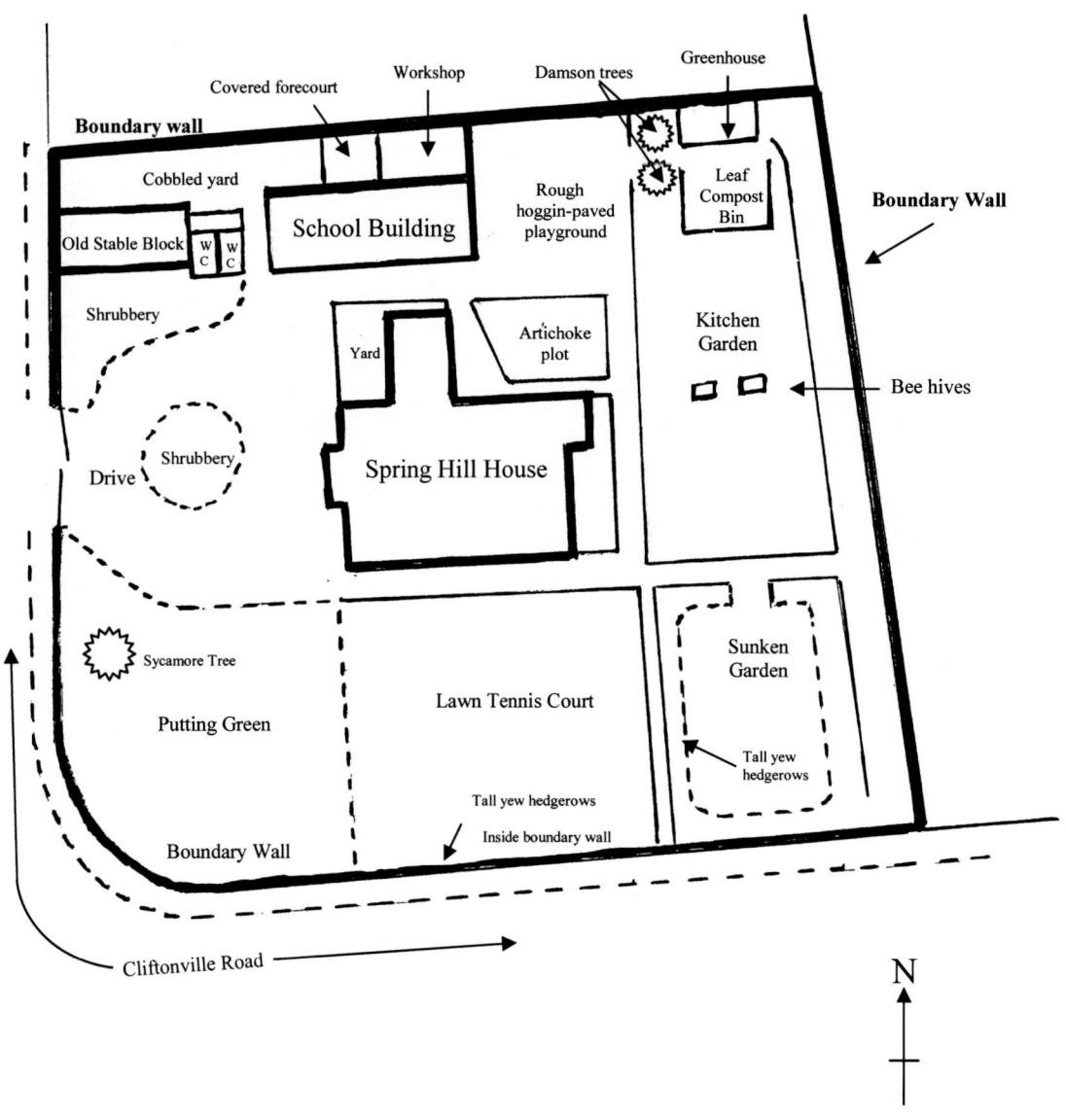

GROUND PLAN

Appendix 7   *The Arnold Way*

Sketches showing the layout of rooms in Spring Hill House
Based on the sketches by George Drewry (1939—1945)
(no attempt made to depict relative sizes or proportions)

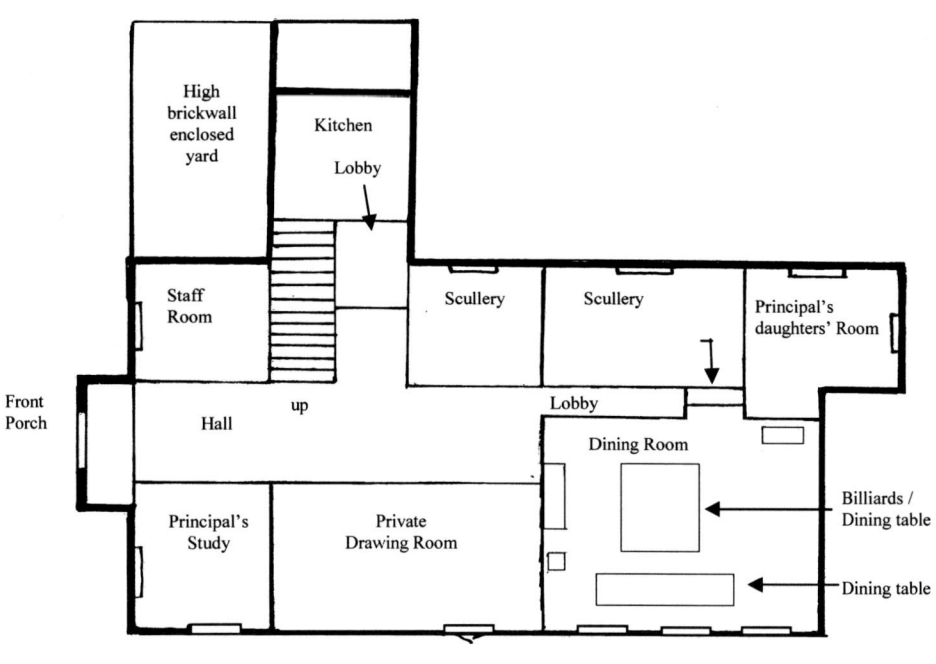

GROUND FLOOR

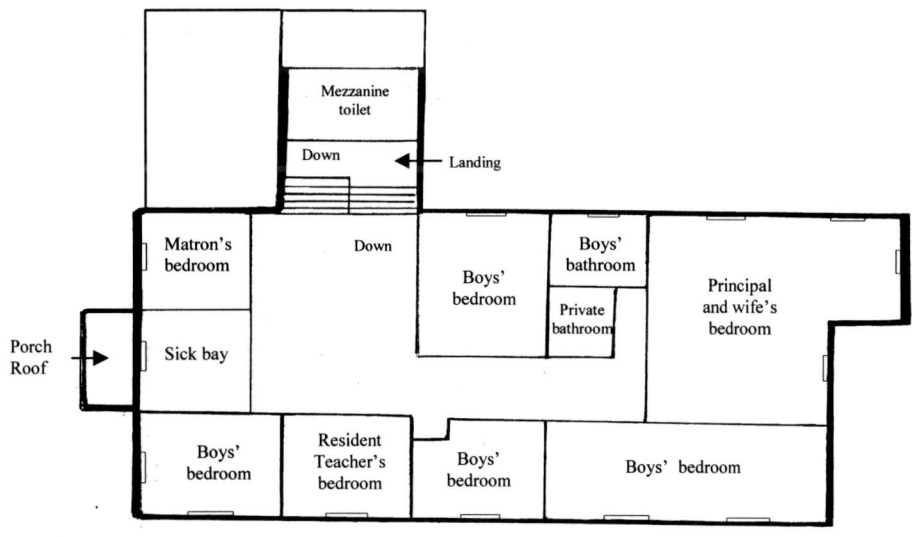

FIRST FLOOR

The Arnold Way   **Appendix 7**

Sketches showing the layout of rooms in the School Building at Spring Hill.

(No attempt is made to depict relative room sizes or proportions)

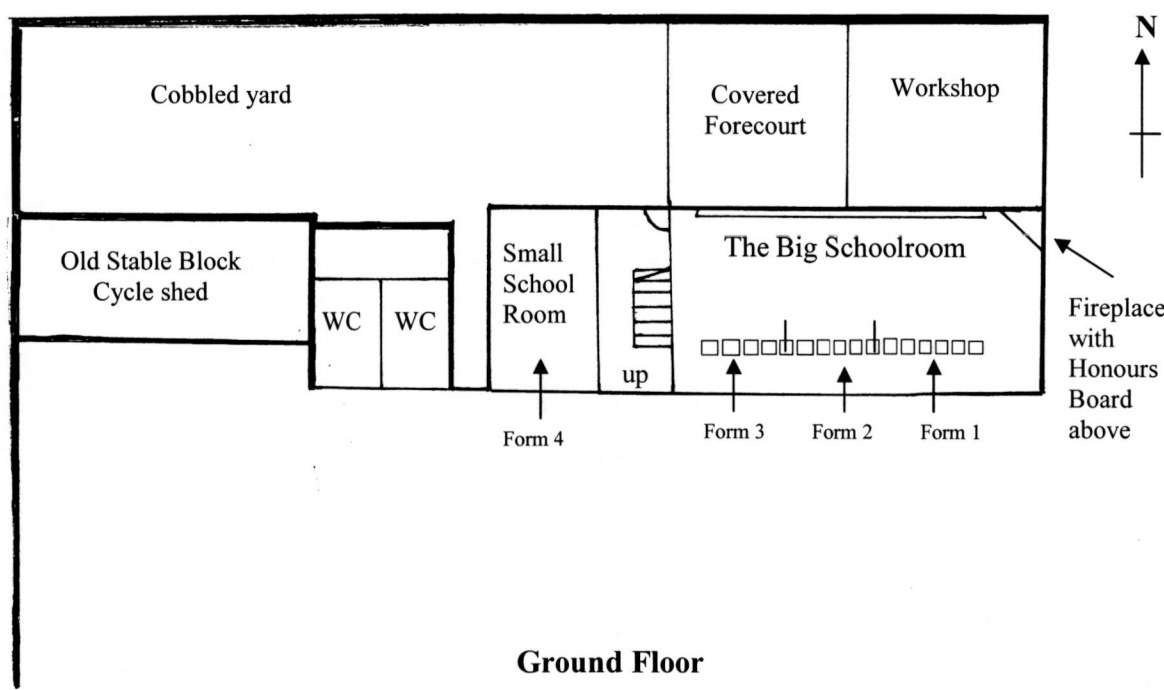

Ground Floor

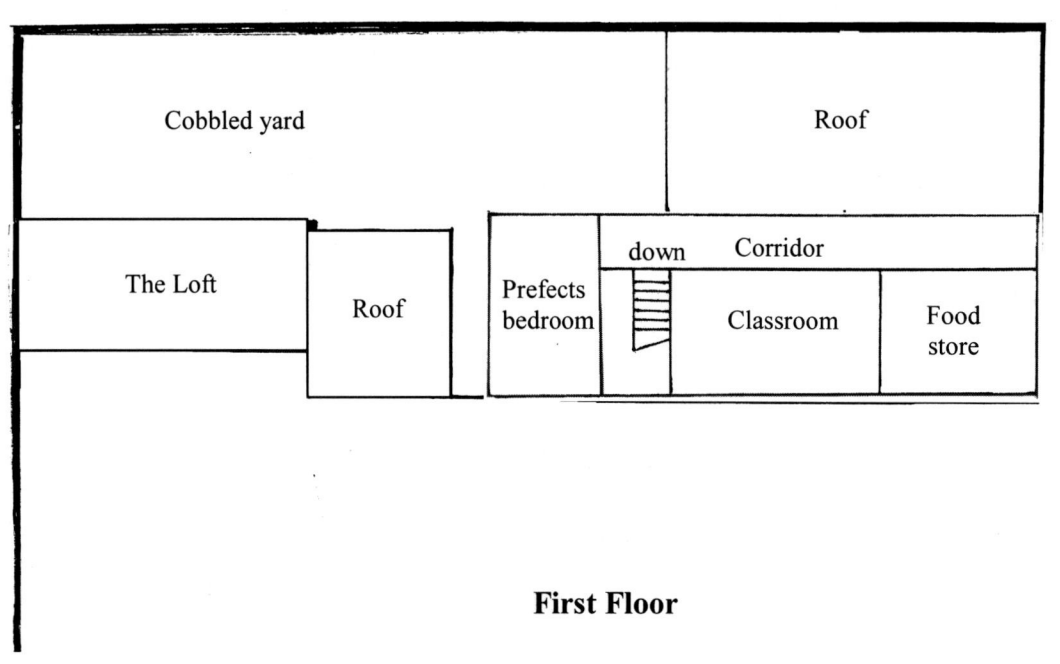

First Floor

Appendix 8

Old Pupils' Contributions.

Some Northampton notes by Abraham Farrar.

The following extracts are taken from *The British Deaf Times* (1913) :-

Northampton is perhaps best known as the centre of the boot and shoe trade, but some of my readers know it as the home of a flourishing private school for the deaf, now in its forty-fifth year, and may recall the fact that there is another Northampton across the water, where also there is a well-known oral institution. (Situated in Massachusetts, U.S.A.)

All Saints' Church, Northampton, 2008

Northampton in 1868 was not the thriving manufacturing town it now is; in fact, it was still enjoying its slumbers as a country town. There were not more than half-a-dozen churches, and of these only four were ancient. On the other hand, there was an unusually large number of Nonconformist chapels, the town having a stronghold of the Dissenters, and, it may be added, of advanced Radicalism, which seems to be in some mysterious way connected with shoemaking. Although a place of considerable antiquity, a great fire in the 17th century destroyed a large part of Northampton, and so as a town it is not interesting. But it still possesses some wonderful monuments of its past. Chief of all is St. Sepulchre's Church, the largest of the four round churches in England; then comes the small but fine Norman Church of St. Peter; Eleanor's Cross, one of several beautiful memorials erected by her sorrowing husband, King Edward I.

Arnold's Chapel has also an interest of its own as an unique example of the conventicler of Puritan days, although somewhat modernised, to say nothing of its associations with Philip Doddridge, the eminent Nonconformist divine of the 18th century.

It would be hard to find an uglier building than All Saints' Church, the principal in the town, with its Roman portico, surmounted by a small figure – just imagine! – of the Merry Monarch, who in some way had benefited the church.

In these days there was a good deal of the old fashioned and kindly intercourse between the clergy and the Nonconformist ministers that was more common than now. The wave of Ritualism had not yet swept over the town. Arnold, being a man of unusually wide and tolerant sympathies, was on excellent terms with all classes. Let me give a few illustrations. It was not unusual for the leading clergyman, the Rev. Sydney Gedge, Vicar of All Saints' to drop in for a chat, and I well remember Mr. and Mrs. Arnold and myself spending an evening with the venerable Vicar of St. Sepulchre's, Mr. Butlin, one of the old school now nearly extinct. Canon Robson, of St. Giles', was also another excellent friend to us; and I must not omit the Roman Catholic clergy, the head of whom, Bishop Amherst, a man of fine presence and great dignity, took a friendly interest in us, as we lived near his cathedral; but I more particularly remember one of his canons, afterwards a Papal Chamberlain, who was on cordial terms with Arnold. He was a noted musician, and freely used his talents in the cause of local charities.

... I may mention a Jewish family, who were deeply interested in Arnold and his pupil; they lived in what was formerly Doddridge's house, and so far recognised this as to present Arnold with a set of original drawings of it for his chapel.

But the most exciting of my experiences of Northampton life was concerned with its politics. Few outside the town now remember the days when the notorious Charles Bradlaugh made it "alive". Arnold took the lead in strongly opposing him as a Parliamentary candidate on account of his atheism, and had a large following amongst those ordinarily Liberals and Radicals, and, as a consequence, incurred much unmerited hatred from the redoubtable Bradlaugh's friends. Bradlaugh's vulgar and coarse abuse of the Christian religion undoubtedly disgusted many good men, but as a politician he was sincere, and possessed of great power over the masses... I shall never forget a great meeting in opposition to Bradlaugh at one of the numerous Parliamentary elections to which I went with Arnold. As seen from the platform it was a veritable inferno of riot, and it was hard to believe men could descend to such depths of passion...

My schooldays over, I was articled to the firm of Messrs. Law and Son, architects and surveyors, in the same town, and continued to reside with Arnold. This was an old established, well-known firm with a large country connection, and everybody in the town considered me fortunate in being admitted as an articled pupil. There was a staff of half a dozen young men, and it was obviously at first a strange experience having a deaf colleague, but they speedily adapted themselves to the new conditions, and never at any time was anything but speech and lip-reading freely used, and only occasionally were unusual or difficult words written down. With Mr. Law himself I was not perhaps so successful in this respect, as he was then of an advanced age – I was his last pupil – and I was not brought much in contact with him. He was a man of fine character and singular geniality, and rarely came into our office without a joke or cheery word for each, and took exceptional interest in my progress. He was a water colour artist of some merit, and one of my valued treasures is a water colour view of Queen Eleanor's Cross, executed by him in the "forties", and given to me by his family after his death.

Appendix 8

Old Pupils' Contributions.

Freddy Davey started to work at the famous Kodak company in 1937 and he sent his article to the Editor of Spring Hill School Magazine in 1940 on his experience with the Kodak firm.

My Work with Kodak Ltd by Freddy Davey.

In the Kodak factory at Harrow, Middlesex, there is a department called Cine Processing. It deals with sub-standard cinematography (films with widths of 16 mm. and 8mm.) It is divided into many services such as:- processing, reducing cinema films of standard width (35 mm.) to 16 and 8 mm., projecting, kodascope library, duplicating, editing and titling.

I work in the editing and titling service in the capacity of artist, doing hand written titles, backgrounds and maps to show routes for customers' films. Here is an example. With a cruising film I start designing a ship in tropical surroundings for a background over which I then do bold lettering composed by the customer, such as:- "Our Cruise in the Mediterranean, August 1939". Finally a colleague photographs the work with a special movie camera with the aid of a photo-flood unit. After having it processed the colleague, if the customer desires, inserts it at the beginning of the film.

Titling plays a very important part in any film. A film is incomplete without titles, otherwise the audience would ask questions – who, where and when?

The art of Titling is also important. When a customer sends us a list of titles to be executed at our discretion, we do them in a pleasing way. The main title, the first thing to be seen on the screen, is done in bold lettering or a fancy or pictorial background with a fade-in and out effect. The sub-titles are in small lettering, same style throughout, on a plain background with no fades. "The End" with a fade-out concludes the film. In this way continuity is built up.

If the customer's film be in colour, we have a stock of colour schemes to meet his requirements harmoniously. For the main title of a garden film I design a close up view of a rose, upon which I write in bold lettering, "Our Garden in Summer 1940". The sub-titles are in the same yellow throughout, but the colour of the patterned background thereof is different. In order to avoid sudden clash of colours the colour of the background of a title must suit that of the scene to follow. For example, if a scene has a green colour predominating, the title will have a green background.

When the war broke out last September, business was at a standstill, due no doubt to the fear of the much talked of blitzkrieg. But a fortnight later up to about a couple of months ago, we were quite busy. During the winter blackout many customers reviewed their old films and noticed they were incomplete. Accordingly they sent us orders for titles and re-conditioning their films. Some were as old as 1930. lately we have been doing practically only A.R.P. and wedding films.

Appendix 8

Old Pupils' Contributions.

Bernard Lewis Pitcher contributed his article to the *Spring Hill Magazine*, December 1936 issue, to reveal his difficulties whilst undergoing the B.Sc. Degree course.

My Work at the Imperial College of Science and Technology
by B.L. Pitcher, B.Sc., Hons. (Lond.)

Ever since I heard that I had realised my ambition of obtaining my degree of Bachelor of Science and the Diploma of A.R.C.S., I have been showered with congratulations of which the number surprised me. I gladly take the opportunity of thanking everyone, especially Old Boys and Masters of Spring Hill for their kind congratulations and good wishes which I very much appreciate.

Although only four years ago, it seems ages since I first went to the College, speculating on what was in store for me. Hundreds of questions flowed through my mind, of which the most important was:- Should I be able to get on somehow? Although I arrived at ten o'clock, the afternoon was more than half spent before I was led to my bench in the chemical laboratory. I found to my relief that there was a very good-tempered student working next to me, who was perfectly willing to help me out of difficulties. I am grateful to him for helping me to tide over the first difficult period when I was a new student.

My chief anxiety at the beginning was about lectures and was somewhat lessened by my father's excellent suggestion that I should take pieces of carbon paper with me and get a student to write carbon copies of lectures for me. I was very fortunate in not only getting a willing student but also a very capable one. He retained his original notes while I kept the carbon copies. The Professors were concerned to know whether I should be able to follow lectures and frequently enquired how I was getting on. They repeatedly requested me to ask them or demonstrators questions as often as I wanted. Indeed they gave me an impression that I did not ask them enough questions. The demonstrators helped me at every opportunity. I am grateful to all who never tired of helping me so much indeed as to set up a kindly atmosphere which made it easier for me to get on.

At first I was able to follow lectures because I had learnt some of the subjects at Spring Hill, but later on they became progressively harder and I had to have recourse to books and had to learn about the Calculus by myself one holiday. In the first two years I found books more helpful than lectures though not so full as the latter. Gradually I came to know students working with me and so was able to pick a willing helper as I drifted from one subject to another. In this way Mr. Richardson, a very clever student, wrote for me in the final years when my subject was Geology. He had learnt much Geology before and so was able to help me a great deal in the last two years. He wrote excellent but concise notes. I shudder to think how I could have got on without his help. In the last half period scarcely a holiday passed without my doing geological field-work, in different parts of England, e.g. South Wales, Gloucestershire, North Cornwall, the Malverns, and I enjoyed it because it did me a lot of good in preventing my health from suffering after the hard work at the College. In one holiday I had to undertake independent field-work as a part of the Degree course on and around the Wrekin in Shropshire, and it took me many weeks.

Needless to say, the work was far from being easy and I had to read lecture notes several times before I could assimilate them, especially in the final years because I was on very advanced grounds in geology which I had never trod before. Now and then I was in despair, wondering whether I could ever get through. Spoken words seemed to have a way of impressing themselves on the mind much better than the written words, for invariably students seemed to understand the practical work after a lecture whereas I sometimes could not make head or tail of it till the evening when I had read the lecture notes several times. Even after this I might have a nebulous idea which gradually grew clearer with a fresh perusal of the notes. Although everybody was perfectly willing to help me, somehow I had an impression that some students did not really understand my difficulties especially after my success in the first few exams, and that they could not realise that I was stone deaf. They seemed to forget that they were continually hearing professors or demonstrators and so unconsciously, whereas the deaf depend on the teachers, books and papers for their language.

Frequently I was asked whether I could lip-read lecturers. I am not a very good lip-reader and frequently have a difficulty in lip-reading professors, students and demonstrators and so have to take recourse to paper and pencil. The lecturers do not always stand facing the audience. They keep on talking even when turning their backs to the audience to write or draw on the blackboard. My friends of course knew of this difficulty but they forgot that I could not lip-read the lecturer and write notes at the same time. The hearing students could follow the lecturer through hearing him and not looking at him while writing notes.

Because I was so slow in absorbing knowledge, I did not have much time for University games and sports although I usually took advantage of the scarce spare time for walks or (in summer) tennis. However, I sometimes attended the meetings at the De La Beche Club (College Geological Club). During one meeting, in common with other members, I put my hand up now and then to signify my approval of a suggestion. Once, just as I was putting up my hand, members around me to my surprise pulled my hand down. Then I learnt that they had just elected me a member of the Club!

In conclusion... I cannot say sufficiently how much I owe to the excellent education I received at Spring Hill School, without which I know I could not have attained such success, for there is nothing like it in Europe.

The Arnold Way   **Appendix 8**

Lithographic Artists (1)

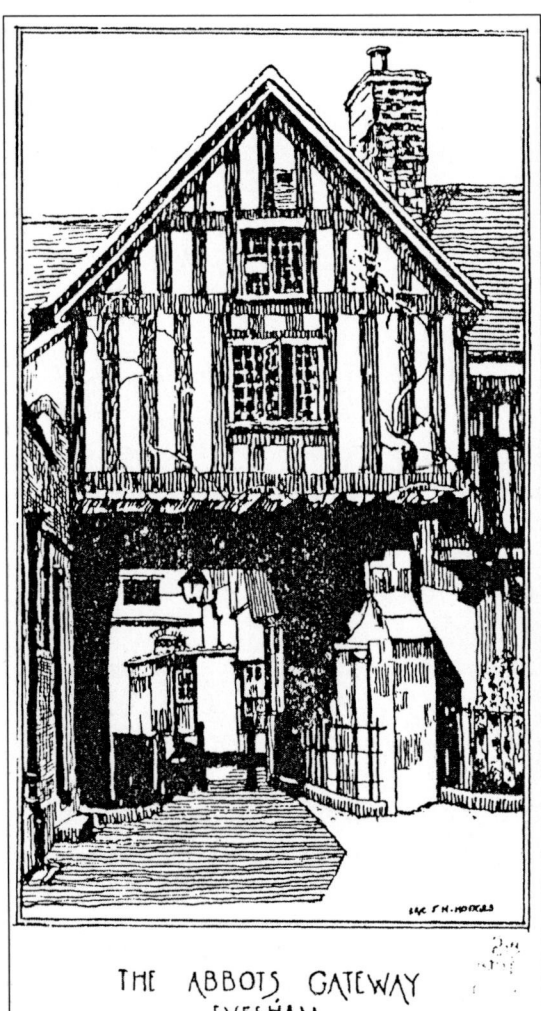

THE ABBOTS GATEWAY EVESHAM

Left: Eric J. H. Hodges from Clacton-on-Sea took the Oxford Junior Local Examinations with honours and distinctions in 1923 at the age of 15 years and the Oxford Senior Certificate in 1925. He attended the School of Architecture and then went into the commercial nursery business. He specialised in lithography and wood-cutting. Eric became a qualified architect in 1940 receiving the A.R.I.B.A. Diploma.

For a picture of Eric J. H. Hodges in a group, see page 25.

Right: Donald Denison from Leeds entered Spring Hill School in 1917 and left in 1928 after passing his Oxford Junior Local Examinations and studied at Leeds College of Art, He made a number of lithographs and woodcuts, some of which were in the Sketch Club Exhibition and College of Art Annual Exhibition held at the Leeds Gallery of Art in November 1931. This was one of his wood-cuts, *Village Green in Linton-in-Green.* Two more examples of Denison's wood-cuts are shown on the next page.

For a picture of Donald Denison in a group, see page 25.

Appendix 8

Lithographic Artists (2)

Runswick Bay, Whitby, December 1939

Scarborough Castle, April 1939

Appendix 8

Old Pupils' Contributions.

Bobby Byers, or Robert A. Byers, worked for the Deaf and Dumb Mission at Durham. He found that employers were sympathetic and kept many of the deaf in constant employment. He *thinks it is a great pity that many of them have not been taught speech and lipreading and are therefore terribly handicapped in life.*

My experiences amongst the Deaf and Dumb by Robert A. Byers.
From *Spring Hill Magazine*, April 1934.

I am a missioner to the deaf and dumb and would like to write about my experiences among them. I have passed examinations for a lay-readership and hold a licence from the Archbishop of York for welfare work amongst the deaf and dumb.

A greater part of the deaf and dumb are of the working-class type and have been brought up in surroundings quite different from those which we have been privileged to enjoy. Many of them are poor and I am sorry to say that their education is sadly below standard. Many are unable to lipread or use the art of speech, hence the prevalence of finger-spelling and signs, their only methods of communication.

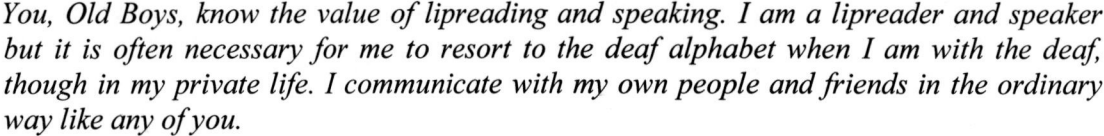
Bobby Byers.

A great number of these unfortunate people need assistance for they cannot help themselves much, though there are a few who can lipread, speak and help themselves more because they are better educated. It is a pity, a heart breaking thing for the ill-educated deaf to be denied the enjoyment of many things in life. They are cut off from the ordinary communications of life and many of them do not read books. Their chief interests are seeing things, such as football matches and films, and spending their leisure in games.

You, Old Boys, know the value of lipreading and speaking. I am a lipreader and speaker but it is often necessary for me to resort to the deaf alphabet when I am with the deaf, though in my private life. I communicate with my own people and friends in the ordinary way like any of you.

I must confess that I find some people difficult to lipread and sometimes I have to use paper and pencil. That's simple!

All we, Old Boys, have a lot to be thankful for, when we realise the benefits we derive from the splendid education we received under the able guidance of the hard working Head and Staff. I know their labours and great patience. We, with the advantage of this training, are able to help ourselves in our daily life.

Illustrations.

Introduction.

    Dr. B. L. Pitcher and author, 1999
    Philip E. Gibbons and his photo albums, 2008
    Lyonel Pritchard
    Map of Northampton Town

Chapter 1.

    21 Primrose Hill, Northampton, 2008
    Thomas Arnold, circa 1870s
    Abraham Farrar, jr., circa 1890s
    Map showing the site of Fairview House, 1885
    Walter S. Bessant
    James Howard's notes on Mary Hardcastle
    Thomas Arnold and 3 female students
    1901 map showing the site of Primrose Hill and St. Paul's Road

Chapter 2.

    25 & 27 St. Paul's Road, Northampton, 2008
    Hugh N. Dixon
    Wickham House, 23 East Park Parade, Northampton
    Cyril Carr
    Noel G. Maddison
    Noel G. Maddison working in the laboratory
    Alan Allsebrook
    1901 map showing the site of Wickham House, East Park Parade

Chapter 3.

    Frederick Ince-Jones
    Spring Hill House in 1912
    Map showing the site of Spring Hill, 1910s
    Alexander Bilibin
    Miss Shackleton and Miss C. King with boys, 1917
    Garden plot
    Lyonel H. Pritchard
    The Dining Room
    Spring Hill Lawn in the 1910s
    The Big Schoolroom in the 1920s
    J. Oliver Cayley
    Wynne Coates and Tom McClure (cartoons)
    Lawn tennis court
    Group of boys, circa 1922
    View of Cliftonville Road, circa 1930.
    Entrance to Spring Hill, 2008
    Mr. Ince-Jones's car Morris Cowley, 1929
    Kenneth H. Pritchard
    Edgar Lewis Mundin
    Strolling in the countryside
    Stanley G. Powell
    N.A.T.D. Conference, Glasgow, 1913
    A group of boys with Mr. Ince-Jones at Spring Hill, 1927
    Spring Hill tennis players, 1928
    Raymond Thorpe
    All Saints' Church, Northampton
    Getting ready for Church

Illustrations (contd)

Raymond Thorpe (cartoon)
Philip Gibbons
Boys posing on the Spring Hill lawn
Jack Hill (cartoon)
Newspaper cuttings on examination successes in 1928/1929

Chapter 4.

Carpentry Class, 1932
Kenneth Pritchard (cartoon)
Spring Hill School Magazines
Alistair Fisher
Three Cheers for the School
Bernard Lewis Pitcher
Miss Helen Keller
Executive Committee of the N.C.T.D., Margate, 1934
Press cuttings on B. L. Pitcher's success, 1937
John Wright
Mr. Ince-Jones's Botany Class
3rd Old Pupils' Reunion, Grosvenor Hotel, London, 1934

Chapter 5.

Cricket on the Castle Ashby Ground, 1931
J. O. Cayley's sketch of the Old Boys' Cricket Team
Patrick Fischer
The Cricketing brothers, Lyonel and Kenneth Pritchard, 1931
The Radford brothers, Glenn and Jack
Jack Attwood and cartoon
Jack Murphy
School Cricket Team, 1930
Old Boys setting out to field
Indoor Swimming Baths, Midsummer Meadow
Boys mowing the lawn tennis court, 1931
Boys putting on the Spring Hill lawn, 1930
Diving at Swimming Baths, Midsummer Meadow
Football Team 1937-1938
Cross-Country Running, 1936
A cycle ride, 1931
Mr. Ince-Jones on a bicycle (cartoon)
Althorp House
Walking along the Blisworth Canal
Senior Boys and their bee hive
Mr. Swann
Lyonel Pritchard on a sledge in snow, 1930
Kenneth Pritchard on a sledge in snow 1930
Ice-skaters
Coach outing
Staff having their lunch
Boys having their lunch
Freddy Davey, cartoonist
"Once Upon a Time" sketch by F. Davey
Enjoying their stroll, 1927
Richard Murphy and Lyonel Pritchard resting at an inn
Sheep-shearing
Pytchley Hunt
A motor coach ready to take boys out
Visit to Shakespeare's Birthplace

Illustrations (contd)

Gunpowder Plot Room, Ashby St. Ledgers, Daventry
Abington Park

Chapter 6.

The Clicking Room, Messrs. Barratt's.
Morris Motor car industry, Cowley, Oxford
Northampton Gasworks
Clark and Sherwells' Printing Firm
David Hyslop
Mr. Melvin, Philip Melvin and Mr. Ince-Jones
George Drewry
George and Ralph Drewry ready for School, 1942
G. Drewry's Prize Certificate, 1939
Weeding time in Spring Hill Garden, July 1942
The last School Group, July 1942
Ginger the School cat
Mr. and Mrs. Mundin
G. Drewry, S. Barkes, R. Drewry, G. Munro
The Ince-Jones family
Boys with HRH Prince William, November 1944
Apple Tree Cottage, Harpole, 2008
Mr. Ince-Jones relaxing by the sea
The last Christmas Card, 1960

Appendix 3. Example from the Oxford School Certificate: English Essay, 1918

Appendix 4. Leaves from the Prospectus, 1910s.
References from the Prospectus, 1930s.

Appendix 5. (a) Spring Hill groups 1925, 1927, 1930, 1938, 1941.
(b) Spring Hill School Cricket Teams 1938, 1941, 1942, 1943
(c) Spring Hill School Football Teams 1937, 1939, 1942, 1944
(d) The Pritchard Photographic Collection
(e) The Philip E. Gibbons Photographic Collection

Appendix 6. Ambrose Isted, Ecton
St. Katharine's Church, Northampton
The Rev. W. B. Sleight
The Deaf Institute, Seymour Place, Northampton
A group of men with Mr. Barnett at St. Mark's Church, Northampton
John Hensman
Address of John Hensman of Spring Hill Cottage, Northampton, 1854
Description of sale and proceeds of Springfield, 1889
1885 map showing Spring Hill

Appendix 7. Sketched plans of Spring Hill Premises

Appendix 8. All Saints' Church, 2008
Eric J. H. Hodges's lithographic sketch of The Abbots Gateway, Evesham
Donald Denison's lithographic sketch of the Village Green in Linton, 1931
Donald Denison's lithographic sketch of Runswick Bay, Whitby, 1939
Donald Denison's lithographic sketch of Scarborough Castle, 1939
Bobby Byers (cartoon)

References

Allsebrook, A.P.: *A Wheel in North Western France, The Silent World*, 1909.
Allsebrook, A.P.: *Letters from the Farther West, The British Deaf Times*, 1911.
Boyce, A.J.: *History of the Yorkshire Residential School for the Deaf*, 1987.
Boyce, A.J. & Lavery, Elaine: *The Lady in Green*, BDHS, 1999.
Boyce, A.J. & Lavery, Elaine: *Through Eyes Not Ears*, BDHS, 2005.
Braddock, Guilbert C.: *Notable Deaf Persons*, 1975.
Dimmock, A.F.: *Tommy*, Scottish Workshop, 1991.
Eichholz, Dr.A.: *A Study of the Deaf in England and Wales 1930 – 1932*, HMSO, 1933.
Farrar, A.: *Exaggerated Statements, British Deaf Monthly*, 1908-09.
Farrar, A.: *The Grand Tour. The British Deaf Times*, 1930.
Ince-Jones, F.: *Awakened,* July 1953 (typed mss ref. ZA 8801), Northamptonshire Record Office.
Jackson, P.W. & Lee, Raymond: *Deaf Lives*, BDHS, 2001.
Jackson, P.W.: *A Pictorial History of Deaf Britain*, 2001.
Lee, Raymond: *A Beginner's Introduction to Deaf History*, BDHS, 2004.
Maugham, W. Somerset: *A Writer's Notebook*, 1949.
Pitcher, B.L.: Newspaper cuttings, 1 – 67. Private collection.
Powell, S.G.: *Mr. Ince-Jones' School for Deaf Boys, The Volta Review*, April 1943.
Pritchard, K.H.: *Mr. Frederick Ince-Jones, The British Deaf Times,* 1954.
Pritchard, L.H.: *The High School for the Deaf, Spring Hill School, Teacher of the Deaf*, 1961.
Thorpe, R. B.: *Torby*, Pub. 1995.
Wright, D.: *A Fox Without a Tail, Encounter Magazine*, April 1958.
Wright, D.: *Deafness, Autobiography*, 1969

Censuses of Northampton 1861, 1871, 1881, 1891, 1901.
Census of Islington 1891.
Census of Ilford 1901.
Directories of Northampton (misc.) from 1850 to 1920.
NATD Conference Proceedings, Edinburgh, 1907.
NATD Conference Proceedings, Glasgow, 1913.
Northampton Daily Chronicle: Presentation to Mr. and Mrs. Dixon. June 1910.
Northampton Herald, 1881 – 1898.
Northampton Independent. School for the Deaf. March 1927.
Northampton Independent: Obituary. Mr. F. Ince-Jones, February 26 1954.
Northampton Mercury, 1874 – 1889.
Northampton Mercury: Obituary of Dr. A.H. Jones. February 1901.
Northampton Tracts, Series.III, no 165. The Rev. Thomas Arnold: *Great Thoughts*, 1896.
Northampton Tracts (4th series), no VIII, 1-8.
Proceedings of Conference of the Governing Bodies of Institutions for the Education of the Deaf, 1881.
Quarterly Review of Deaf Mute Education. Vol. IV, no. 46, April 1897.
Royal School for the Deaf Magazine, Margate. 1934.
Spring Hill School Magazine issues. 1930 to 1945.
Spring Hill School. Report & correspondence. Public Record Office. 1943-44. Ref. 33/157.
Teacher of the Deaf issues. 1903 – 1954.
Teacher of the Deaf : Analytical Chemistry for the Deaf. 1904 /1907.
The British Deaf Monthly issues. 1896 – 1903.
The British Deaf Times issues. 1903 – 1945.
The British Deaf Times: Mr. Noel G. Maddison. 1908.
The British Deaf Times: Obituaries: Mr. H.N. Dixon and A. Farrar, 1944.

References (contd)

<u>Deaf History Journal. issues 1997 – 2004</u>

Boyce, A.J.: *The Deaf Squire of Ecton*, DHJ. Vol.2.1 Aug 1998.
Boyce, A.J.: *The Thomas Arnold Memorials,* DHJ. Vol.1.1. April 1997.
Boyce, A.J.: *Spurs Deaf Club*, DHJ. Vol. 7.3. April 2004.
Boyce, A.J.: Pollard,R. & H.: *Flying High,* DHJ. Vol. 8.2. Dec. 2004.
Dimmock, A.F.: *Obituaries: Raymond Thorpe and Doreen Auger,* DHJ. Vol.1.2. Aug 1997.
Hay, J.A.: *Bernard L. Pitcher,* DHJ Supplement V. Aug 1999.
Jackson, P.W.: *Dr. Wallis and the Little Boy*, DHJ. Vol.3.2. April 2004.
Stewart,I.: *The Centenary of the Death of Thomas Arnold,* DHJ. Vol.1.1 April 1997.

<u>Publications of the Rev. Thomas Arnold</u>

Arnold, T.: *Analogies of the language of sound and touch*, n.d.
Arnold, T.: *Defects and impediments of the organs of speech*, 1893.
Arnold, T.: *Education of Deaf Mutes*, 2 vols. 1888 – 1891.
Arnold, T.: *Translation of Prof. Dupont's review of Arnold's Teacher manual*, n.d.
Arnold, T.: *Education of the Deaf and Dumb. An exposition of the French and German systems,* 1872.
Arnold, T.: *Languages of the Senses with special reference to the Education of the Deaf, Blind, Deaf and Blind,* 1894.
Arnold, T.: *Lipreading for the Deaf,* 1982.
Arnold, T.: *Method of Teaching the Deaf and Dumb Speech, Lipreading and Language*, 1881.
Arnold, T.: *On the Preparatory Training of Deaf Mutes*, 1886.
Arnold, T.: *Prevention of Signs among Junior Pupils*, 1886.
Arnold, T.: *Reminiscences of Forty Years,* 1895.